1000 FACTS ON
WORLD
GEOGRAPHY

First published by Miles Kelly Publishing Ltd
Bardfield Centre, Great Bardfield
Essex, CM7 4SL

Copyright © 2001 Miles Kelly Publishing
Some material in this book first appeared in 1000 Things You Should Know

2 4 6 8 10 9 7 5 3 1

Editor
Belinda Gallagher

Assistant Editor
Mark Darling

Art Director
Clare Sleven

Design
Whitelight

Picture Research
Liberty Newton

British Library Cataloguing-in-Publication Data
A catalogue record for this book is available from the British Library

ISBN 1-84236-044-2

Printed in Hong Kong

www.mileskelly.net
info@mileskelly.net

1000 FACTS ON
WORLD GEOGRAPHY

John Farndon
Consultant Keith Irvine

Miles Kelly

PUBLISHING

Contents

Key

 Asia

 The Americas

 Europe

 Africa and Australasia

 People

 Places

Contents

Contents

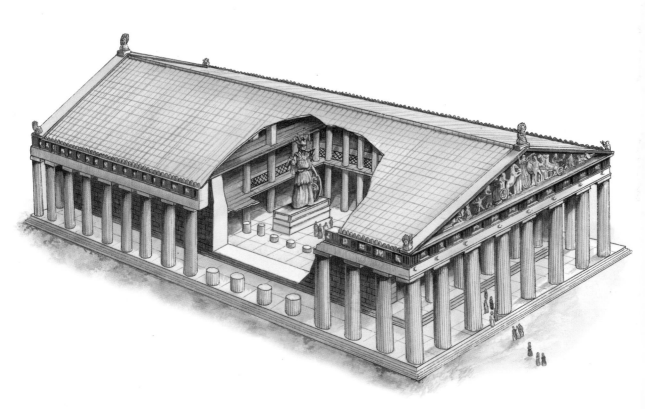

Canada

▲ *The completion of the Canadian Pacific railroad right across Canada in 1885 was one of the great engineering feats of the 1800s.*

- **Capital:** Ottawa. Area: 9,970,610 sq km. Currency: Canadian dollar. Languages: French and English.

- **Physical features:** Highest mountain: Mt Logan (5951 m). Longest river: the Mackenzie, linked to the Peace by the Great Slave Lake (4241 km).

- **Population:** 30.3 million. Population density: 3/sq km. Life expectancy: men 76.1 years; women 81.8 years.

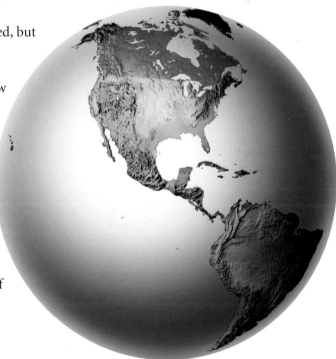

- **Wealth:** GDP: $608 billion. GDP per head: $19,640.

- **Exports:** Vehicles and parts, machinery, petroleum, aluminium, timber, wood pulp, wheat.

- **Canada** is the world's second largest country.

- **Three-quarters** of Canada's small population live within 100 km of the southern border with the USA; the rest of the country is rugged and only thinly inhabited.

- **Only 7%** of Canada is farmed, but this is a big area. The Prairie provinces – Saskatchewan, Alberta and Manitoba – grow a lot of wheat and raise many cattle.

- **Canada** has 10% of the world's forest and is the world's largest exporter of wood products and paper.

- **The Inuit people** of the far north in the Arctic were given their own homeland of Nunavut in 1999.

9

The USA

- **Capital:** Washington DC. Area: 9,372,610 sq km. Currency: US dollar. Language: English.
- **Physical features:** Highest mountain: Mt McKinley (6,194 m). Longest river: the Mississippi-Missouri-Red Rock (6,019 km).
- **Population:** 278.1 million. Population density: 29/sq km. Life expectancy: men 73.4 years; women 80.1 years.
- **Wealth:** GDP: $7783 billion. GDP per head: $29,080.
- **Exports:** Aircraft, vehicles, chemicals, machinery, electronic goods, coal, oil, maize, wheat, soya beans.
- **Native Americans lived** in North America for 15,000 years before the Europeans arrived in the 16th century and gradually drove westwards, brushing the Native Americans aside. In 1788, English colonists founded the United States of America, now the world's oldest democratic republic, with a famous constitution (set of laws).
- **The USA** is the world's fourth largest country in area, third largest in population, and has the largest GDP.
- **In the 1950s and 60s** Americans earned more money, ate more food, used more energy and drove more cars than anyone else in the world.
- **Now the USA** is the world's prime consumer of energy, oil, copper, lead, zinc, aluminium, corn, coffee and cocoa. It is also prime producer of corn and aluminium, and one of the top five producers of energy, oil, copper, lead, zinc, wheat and sugar.

◄ *In the US, the bald eagle symbolizes liberty and hope.*

...**FASCINATING FACT**...
One in two Americans owns a computer – more than any other country in the world.

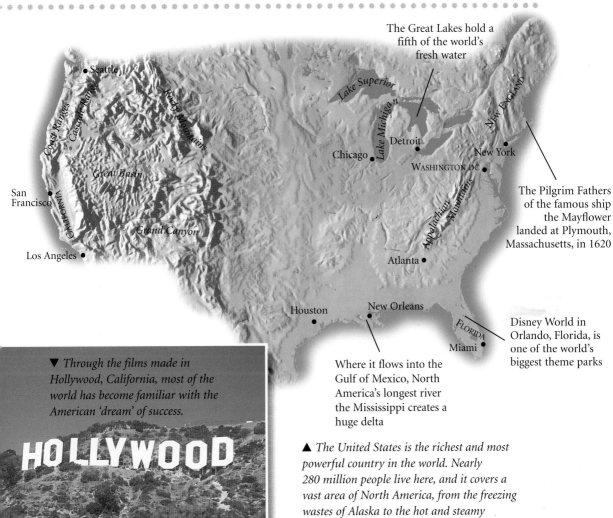

The Great Lakes hold a fifth of the world's fresh water

Lake Superior

Lake Michigan

Seattle

Rocky Mountains

Cascade Range

Coast Ranges

NEW ENGLAND

Detroit

Chicago

New York

WASHINGTON DC

Great Basin

San Francisco

CALIFORNIA

Appalachian Mountains

The Pilgrim Fathers of the famous ship the Mayflower landed at Plymouth, Massachusetts, in 1620

Grand Canyon

Los Angeles

Atlanta

Houston

New Orleans

FLORIDA

Miami

Disney World in Orlando, Florida, is one of the world's biggest theme parks

▼ *Through the films made in Hollywood, California, most of the world has become familiar with the American 'dream' of success.*

HOLLYWOOD

Where it flows into the Gulf of Mexico, North America's longest river the Mississippi creates a huge delta

▲ *The United States is the richest and most powerful country in the world. Nearly 280 million people live here, and it covers a vast area of North America, from the freezing wastes of Alaska to the hot and steamy Everglades (marshes) of Florida.*

11

West Coast USA

▲ *Sunset Boulevard in LA is a 30 km long road. Its Sunset Strip section is popular with film stars.*

- **The western USA** is mountainous, with peaks in the Rockies, Cascades and Sierra Nevada soaring over 4000 m.

- **Seattle** is the home of computer software giant Microsoft, and Boeing, the world's biggest aircraft maker.

- **Seattle** is also the home of the Starbucks café chain – made famous by the TV series *Frasier*.

- **Los Angeles** (LA) sprawls over a larger area than any other city in the world and has endless kilometres of freeways.

- **Film-makers** came to the LA suburb of Hollywood in 1907 because of California's sunshine. It has been the world's greatest film-making centre ever since.

- **The San Andreas fault** is the boundary between two huge continental plates. As it moves it gives west coast cities earthquakes. The worst may be yet to come.

... **FASCINATING FACT** ...
Silicon Valley near San Francisco has the world's greatest concentration of electronics firms.

▲ *California's Golden Gate Bridge, built in 1937, was the world's longest suspension bridge until 1964. It spans 1280 m and its towers soar an amazing 227 m above the waters of San Francisco Bay. Its total length is 2737 m.*

- **San Francisco's** Golden Gate is named after the 1849 rush when prospectors came in thousands to look for gold.

- **California** is known as the 'Sunshine State'.

- **California's** San Joaquin valley is a major wine-growing region.

Yellowstone Park

▲ *Yellowstone Park helps protect bison, many of which were slaughtered in the 1800s as a way of suppressing Indians who depended on them for their living.*

- **Yellowstone** is the oldest and best-known national park in the USA. It was established by Act of Congress on March 1, 1872.

- **It is one of the world's largest** parks covering 8983 sq km of rugged mountains and spectacular deep valleys.

- **It is situated** across Wyoming, Montana and Idaho.

- **Yellowstone** is famous for its lakes and rivers such Yellowstone Lake and Snake River.

- **Most of Yellowstone** is forested in lodgepole pines, along with other conifers, cottonwoods and aspens. It also has a wealth of wild flowers.

- **Yellowstone's** wild animals include bison, elk, bighorn sheep, moose, grizzly bears and wolves.

- **Yellowstone** has the world's greatest concentration of geothermal features including 10,000 hot springs and 200 geysers, as well as steam vents, mud cauldrons, fumaroles and paint pots.

- **The most famous geyser** is Old Faithful, which spouts every hour or so. The biggest is the 115 m Steamboat.

- **One of the biggest** volcanic eruptions ever occured in Yellowstone Park two million years ago. Enough lava poured out in one go to build six Mt Fujiyamas.

- **There are signs** that Yellowstone may soon erupt as a 'supervolcano' – an eruption on an unimaginable scale.

▲ *Yellowstone sits on top of a volcanic hot spot which gives it its famous geysers and hot springs – and may make it the site of the biggest eruption of all time.*

Midwest USA

- **Huge amounts** of wheat and maize are grown on the damper eastern side of the vast rolling plains.

- **Millions** of beef cattle are raised on ranches in the drier west.

- **The weather is often** extreme here, with scorching summer days and winter blizzards.

- **Tornado Alley** is a strip of land through Kansas and beyond which is blasted by hundreds of tornadoes every summer.

- **Heavy farming** in the 1930s let dry winds strip away soil leaving just dust over a vast area called the Dust Bowl. Irrigation and windbreaks have lessened the problem.

- **Millions of buffalo (bison)** roamed the Great Plains 200 years ago. Now just 50,000 live on reserves.

▼ *Chicago is famous for its skyscrapers. It is also known for being the home of Al Capone, leader of the South Side gang in the 1920s.*

▲ *The midwest is North America's agricultural heartland, raising millions of cattle and growing vast areas of yellow corn.*

- **Detroit** on the Great Lakes is the centre of the US car and truck industry. Ford, Chrysler and General Motors all have their headquarters here.

- **Detroit** is sometimes known as Motown (short for 'motor town') and was famous in the 1960s for its black soul 'Motown' music.

- **Many Italians** have emigrated to the USA and most US cities have an Italian area. Chicago's Italians invented their own deep, soft version of the pizza.

- **Chicago,** known as 'The Windy City', is the USA's third largest city, home to over three million people.

New England

- **New England** is six states in northeast USA – Maine, Vermont, New Hampshire, Massachusetts, Rhode Island and Connecticut.

- **New England** was one of the first areas of North America settled by Europeans in the 1600s.

- **The USA's** oldest buildings are in New England.

▶ *Harvard University, Boston, is the oldest institution of higher learning in the US.*

- **New England** is famous for its attractive small towns with pretty 18th- and 19th-century white clapperboard houses, and its elegantly spired churches.

- **Vermont's** name means 'green mountain' and it has fewer urban inhabitants than any other state.

- **Basketball** was invented in Massachusetts in 1891.

- **Route 128** in Massachusetts is famed for its cutting-edge electronic technology factories.

- **Boston** is one of the USA's oldest, most cultured cities. It also has a large number of educational and research institutes. Harvard University is at Cambridge nearby. Yale is in Connecticut.

- **New Hampshire** is well-known for its scenery.

▲ *New England is famous for the stunning colours of its trees in 'fall' (autumn), when the leaves turn to red, gold and amber.*

...**FASCINATING FACT**...
Rhode Island is the smallest state in the USA, which is why it is often called 'Little Rhody'.

19

New York

- **New York City** is the largest city in the USA and one of the largest in the world, with a population of 7.5 million.

- **Over 18 million people** live in the New York metropolitan area.

- **New York has five** main boroughs: Manhattan, Brooklyn, the Bronx, Queens and Staten Island.

- **Manhattan** is the oldest part of the city, but now has its tallest skyscrapers, including the Empire State Building (1931), for 40 years the world's tallest building at 381 m.

- **The 411 m high** World Trade Center is one of the world's tallest buildings.

- **New York's most famous** statue is the Statue of Liberty, erected in 1886 at the entrance to New York harbour.

- **Dutch settler** Peter Minuit is said to have bought Manhattan island from the Iroquois Indians for $24.

> ....FASCINATING FACT....
> New York is the USA's largest port,
> its trade centre and the finance centre
> of the world.

▶ *The Empire State Building is the 'eighth wonder' of the modern world. It is both a commercial skyscraper, with over 900 tenants, and a symbol of New York.*

▼ *The skyscrapers of Manhattan give New York one of the most famous skylines in the world.*

- **New York** began in 1625 as the Dutch settlement of New Amsterdam. It was renamed New York when the English took over in 1664.

- **New York's famous** finance centre Wall Street is named after a protective wall built by Dutch colonists in 1653.

21

Grand Canyon

- **The Grand Canyon** in Arizona in the southwest USA is one of the most spectacular gorges in the world.

- **The Grand Canyon** is about 450 km long and varies in width from less than 1 km to over 30 km.

- **In places** the Grand Canyon is so narrow that motorcycle stunt riders have leaped right across from one side to the other.

- **The Grand Canyon** is about 1600 m deep, with almost sheer cliff sides in some places.

▼ *Completed in 1936, and formerly called Boulder Dam, the Hoover Dam was renamed in 1947 to honour President Hoover.*

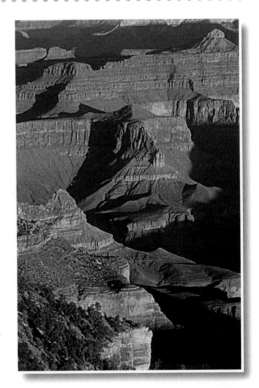

- **Temperatures** at the bottom of the Canyon can be as much as 14°C hotter than they are at the top, and the bottom of the Canyon gets only 180 mm of rain per year compared to 660 mm at the top.

- **The Grand Canyon** was cut by the Colorado River over millions of years as the whole Colorado Plateau was rising bit by bit. The bends in the river's course were shaped when it still flowed over the flat plateau on top, then the river kept its shape as it cut down through the rising plateau.

- **As the Colorado** cut down, it revealed layers of limestone, sandstone, shale and other rocks in the cliffs.

▲ *The shadows cast by the evening sun reveal the layer upon layer of rock in the steep sides of the Grand Canyon.*

- **The Colorado** is one of the major US rivers, 2334 km long.

- **The Hoover Dam** across the Colorado is one of the world's highest concrete dams, 221 m high.

- **The Hoover Dam** creates the 185 km long Lake Mead, North America's biggest artificial lake.

23

Southern USA

- **The south central states** such as Texas, Oklahoma and New Mexico produce a lot of oil and gas.

- **Texas** produces more oil than any other state apart from Alaska.

- **Two of the world's** largest oil companies, Exxon and Amoco, were founded on Texan oil.

- **Texas** is known as the Lone Star state.

- **Louisiana** is known as the Sugar state because it grows so much sugar.

▲ *The growing and selling of cotton is still a major source of income for southern USA.*

▲ *Texas's wealth came with the discovery of oil in 1901. Now aerospace and high-tech industries are thriving in this sunny state.*

- **Oil wealth and aerospace** have attracted high-tech industries to Texan cities such as Dallas, Houston and San Antonio.

- **Cotton** is grown on the Mississippi plains, while tobacco is important in the Carolinas and Virginia.

- **In the mid 1800s** the southern states grew 80% of the world's cotton, largely using black slave labour.

- **Florida** is famous for Disneyworld, the Cape Canaveral space centre and the Everglades, a vast area of steamy tropical swamp infested by alligators.

> ···**FASCINATING FACT**···
> Dallas has the largest commercial airport
> in the world and the most rich people.

Peoples of North America

- **80%** of the population of North America are white descendants of immigrants from Europe.

- **Among the smaller groups** 12% are black, 3% are Asian and 1% are American Indians.

- **Hispanics** are descended from a mix of white, black and American Indian people from Spanish-speaking countries of Latin America such as Mexico, Puerto Rico and Cuba. 9% of the US population is Hispanic.

- **92%** of the population of the USA was born there. Many new immigrants are Hispanic.

- **The original peoples** of North America were the American Indians who were living here for thousands of years before Europeans arrived.

◀ *The original peoples of North America were the Indians, but they have been overwhelmed by European settlers.*

- **The native people** of America were called Indians by the explorer Christopher Columbus, but they have no collective name for themselves. Most American Indians prefer to be identified by tribe.

- **There are about** 540 tribes in the USA. The largest are the Cherokee, Chuppewa, Choctaw, Navajo and Sioux.

- **Most black Americans** are descendants of Africans brought here as slaves from 1600 to 1860.

- **Most European** immigrants were from Britain, so the main language is English.

- **Spanish** is spoken by many Americans and French is spoken by most Canadians.

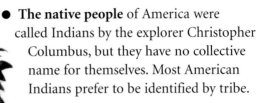

◄ *A Sioux chief. Many Sioux Indians were killed by US cavalry in the massacre at Wounded Knee in 1890.*

American food

▲ *The humble apple pie has come to represent all that is wholesome about America, and has given rise to the saying 'As American as apple pie'.*

● **Many American** foods were brought from Europe by immigrants.

● **Hamburgers** were brought to the USA by German immigrants in the 1800s, but are now the most famous American food.

● **Frankfurters** came from Frankfurt in Germany. They were christened 'hot dogs' by journalist Thomas Dorgan when a stall selling them in a roll opened on New York's Coney Island in 1916.

28

- **The pizza** came from Naples in Italy, but the first pizzeria opened in New York in 1905. Pizzas caught on after 1945.

- **Legend says** the bagel began in Vienna in 1683 as a stirrup-shaped bun made in honour of John III of Poland's horseback defence of the city against the Turks. It was taken to New York by Jewish immigrants.

- **Self-service** cafeterias began in the 1849 San Francisco Gold Rush.

- **The world's first** fast food restaurant may have been the White Castle which opened in Wichita, Kansas in 1921.

- **The world's biggest** fast-food chain is McDonalds which has nearly 20,000 branches worldwide.

- **Pies** have been popular in the US since colonial times, and apple pie is the symbol of American home cooking.

- **American home cooking** includes beef steaks, chicken and ham with potatoes plus a salad. But Americans eat out often – not only fast-food such as hamburgers and French fries, but Chinese, Italian and Mexican dishes.

▲ *The American hamburger has been spread around the world by fast-food chains. The USA consumes 45,000 hamburgers every minute!*

29

Central America

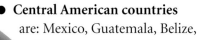

- **Central American countries** are: Mexico, Guatemala, Belize, Honduras, El Salvador, Nicaragua, Costa Rica and Panama.

  - **Mexico:** Capital: Mexico City. Population: 94.3 million. Currency: Peso. Language: Spanish.

  - **Mexico City** is the world's largest city with a population of over 20 million.

  - **Most Central American** countries were torn apart by revolution and civil war in the 1900s, but are now quiet.

- **Mexico owes** more money in foreign debt than any country but Brazil (almost $150 billion) and pays over $37 billion a year back to other countries.

- **Much land** is used for 'cash crops' (crops that can be sold abroad for cash) such as coffee rather than for food.

- **Many Central Americans** work the land, growing food for themselves or labouring on plantations.

- **Maize** (corn) has been grown in Mexico for 7000 years to make things such as tortillas (cornflour pancakes).

Mexico

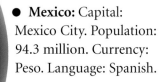

Guatemala

Belize

Honduras

El Salvador

Nicaragua

Costa Rica

Panama

▲ *The Panama Canal cuts right across Central America to link the Atlantic and Pacific Oceans and save ships huge journeys.*

- **Bananas** are the most important export in Central American countries, forming a third of Honduras's entire exports. While bananas are grown on lowlands, coffee beans are important exports for highland regions, especially in Nicaragua, Guatemala, Costa Rica and El Salvador.

- **Most of Mexico's people** are mestizos, descendants of both Spanish settlers and American Indians.

Mexico

- **Capital:** Mexico City.
  Area: 1,972,545 sq km.
  Currency: Mexican peso.
  Language: Spanish.

- **Physical features:** Highest
  mountain: Citlaltépetl
  (5700 m). Longest river:
  Rio Bravo (2100 km).

- **Population:** 94.3 million.
  Population density:
  47/sq km. Life expectancy:
  men 69.5 years; women
  75.5 years.

- **Wealth:** GDP: $348.6
  billion. GDP per head: $3700.

▲ *Mexico lies immediately south of the USA, between the Gulf of Mexico and the Pacific.*

- **Exports:** Petroleum, vehicles, machinery, cotton,
  coffee, fish, fertilizers, minerals.

- **Mexico** is quite mountainous and only 12%
  of the land is suitable for farming, but the
  soil that develops on lava poured out by
  Mexico's many volcanoes is very fertile. Where there
  is enough rain, there are big plantations for tobacco,
  coffee, cane, cocoa, cotton and rubber.

- **Over half Mexico's** export earnings come from
  manufactured goods – notably cars.

- **Mexico has** a rapidly growing population. The birth rate is high and half the population is under 25.

- **Most of Mexico's people** are mestizos – descended from both American Indians and Europeans. But there are still 15 million American Indians.

- **Mexico City** is one of the world's biggest, busiest, dirtiest cities. The urban area has a population of over 20 million – and it is growing rapidly as more people move in from the country to find jobs.

◀ *The Gulf of Mexico formed approximately 200 million years ago when North America broke away from South America and Africa.*

33

The West Indies

▲ *Jamaica's beautiful beaches and all-year-round mild climate have helped make tourism one of Jamaica's leading economic activities.*

● **Cuba:** Capital: Havana. Population: 10.9 million. Currency: Cuban peso. Language: Spanish.

● **Jamaica:** Capital: Kingston. Population: 2.5 million. Currency: Jamaican dollar. Language: English.

● **The four largest islands** in the West Indies are Cuba, Hispaniola, Jamaica and Puerto Rico. Hispaniola is split into two countries: Haiti and the Dominican Republic.

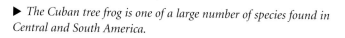

▶ *The Cuban tree frog is one of a large number of species found in Central and South America.*

- **The islands** are mostly in a long curve stretching from Cuba to Trinidad. The Greater Antilles are the islands of the western end. The Lesser Antilles are the eastern end.

- **The original inhabitants** of the West Indies were Carib and Arawak peoples. Most died soon after the Spanish arrived in the 1500s from disease and abuse.

- **Today most West Indians** are descended from Africans brought here as slaves to work on the sugar plantations.

- **The slaves** were freed in the mid-1800s, but most people here are still poor and work for low wages.

- **In Haiti** only one person in 250 has a car; fewer than one in ten has a phone.

- **Half** the people work the land. Many work on sugar, banana or coffee plantations, and also farm a plot to grow their own food.

- **Many tourists** come for the warm weather and clear blue seas.

Venezuela
and neighbours

- **Venezuela:** Capital: Caracas. Population: 22.8 million. Currency: Bolivar. Language: Spanish.

- **Colombia:** Capital: Bogota. Population: 40 million. Currency: Colombian peso. Language: Spanish.

- **Guyana:** Capital: Georgetown. Population: 825,000. Currency: Guyana dollar. Language: English.

Venezuela

Colombia

Guyana

Surinam

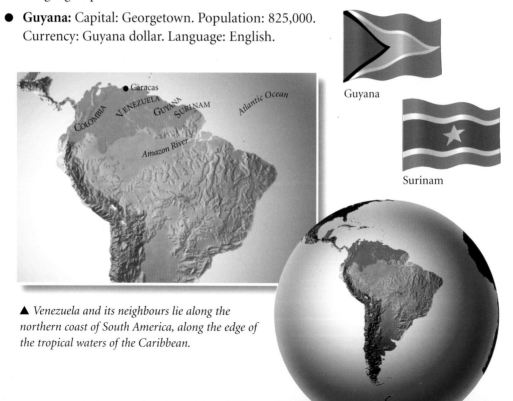

▲ *Venezuela and its neighbours lie along the northern coast of South America, along the edge of the tropical waters of the Caribbean.*

◀ *The Angel Falls plummet into a valley in the spectacular Canaima wilderness area of Venezuela.*

- **Surinam:** Capital: Paramaribo. Population: 425,000. Currency: Surinam guilder. Language: Dutch.

- **French Guiana:** Capital: Cayenne. Population: 114,000. Currency: French franc. Language: French.

- **The discovery of oil** in Venezuela's Lake Maracaibo in 1917 turned Venezuela from one of South America's poorest countries to one of its richest.

- **The Venezuelan city** of Merida has the world's highest cable car, going up 4765 m.

- **The world's highest waterfall** is the Angel Falls in Venezuela, plunging 980 m.

- **The Yanomami** are native peoples who survive in remote forest regions of Venezuela and live by hunting with spears and gathering roots and fruit.

- **Kourou** in French Guiana is the launch site for European spacecraft such as the *Ariane*.

Brazil

◀ *Brazil is the world's fifth largest country, but most people live on the eastern edge. Much of the central area is cerrado (grass wilderness) or thick Amazon rainforest.*

● **Capital:** Brasilia. Area: 8,512,000 sq km. Currency: Real. Language: Portuguese.

● **Physical features:** Highest mountain: Neblina (3014 m). Longest river: the Amazon (6439 km).

● **Population:** 163.7 million. Population density: 19/sq km. Life expectancy: men 63.1 years; women 71 years.

● **Wealth:** GDP: $820 billion. GDP per head: $4790.

● **Exports:** Iron ore, coffee, fruit, timber, sugar, vehicles, beef.

● **Brazil has the biggest** national debt of any country in the world – not far short of $200 billion.

● **Brazil** is the world's biggest coffee grower. Soya, sugarcane, cotton, oranges, bananas and cocoa are also major crops.

● **The city of São Paulo** has grown faster than any other big city in the world and now 17 million people live there. Housing shortages in cities such as Rio de Janeiro and São Paulo mean over 20 million Brazilians live in rickety sheds in sprawling shanty towns called *favelas*.

▲ *São Paulo is the largest city in Brazil and is the capital of the richest and most populated region of Brazil, also São Paulo.*

- **Brazilians are soccer-mad** and have won the World Cup more times than any other country.

- **The Amazon basin** contains the world's largest area of virgin rainforest – but an area almost the size of Ireland is being cleared each year for short-term cattle ranching.

39

The Amazon

▲ *The golden arrow poison frog lives in Central and South American rainforests.*

- **The Amazon River** in South America is the world's second longest river (6439 km), and carries far more water than any other river.

- **The Amazon basin** – the area drained by the Amazon and its tributaries – covers over seven million sq km and contains the world's largest tropical rainforest.

- **Temperatures** in the Amazon rainforest stay about 27°C all year round.

- **The Amazon rainforest** contains more species of plant and animal than anywhere else in the world.

- **The Amazon is home** to about 30,000 different plants, 1500 kinds of bird, and 3000 species of fish in its rivers.

- **Manaus** in the Amazon basin has a population of over a million and a famous 19th century opera house.

- **Since the 1960s** the Brazilian government has been building highways and airports in the forest.

- **10%** of the forest has been lost for ever as trees are cut for wood, or to clear the way for mining and ranching.

- **Forest** can sometimes regrow, but has far fewer species.

▼ *The Amazon river winds its way through the dense rainforest. During the rainy season the river flows slowly, often spilling its banks and flooding large areas of forest.*

...FASCINATING FACT...
The Amazon basin is home to
30 million different kinds of insect.

Peru and neighbours

- **Peru:** Capital: Lima. Area: 1,285,216 sq km. Currency: Nuevo Sol. Languages: Spanish and Quechua.

  - **Physical features:** Highest mountain: Huascaran (6768 m). Longest river: The Amazon (6,439 km).

    - **Population:** 24.4 million. Population density: 18/sq km. Life expectancy: men 65.9 years; women 70.9 years.

      - **Wealth:** GDP: $63.7 billion. GDP per head: $2610.

        - **Exports:** Copper, lead, fish products, iron, zinc, oil, coffee, llama and alpaca wool, cotton.

  - **Peru** is the third largest country in South America. The coastal plain is desert, but Peru's biggest city Lima is here. Inland are the towering Andes mountains, where rivers have cut deep gorges.

- **Peru** was the home of the Inca Empire conquered by the Spaniard Francisco Pizarro in the 1520s. Now it has a larger Indian population than any other South American nation.

▲ *The llama was for centuries the main source of meat and wool, and the main means of transport for people in Peru.*

- **Peru** is a leading producer of copper, lead, silver and zinc, and a major fishing nation. But most people are poor, especially in the mountains. In the 1990s guerillas called Sendero Luminoso (Shining Path) and Tupac Amaru sparked off violent troubles.

- **Ecuador:** Capital: Quito. Population: 11.9 million. Currency: Sucre. Language: Spanish.

- **Bolivia:** Capital: La Paz. Population: 7.8 million. Currency: Sucre. Language: Spanish.

▶ *The ruined ancient Inca city of Machu Picchu stands high in the Andes Mountains.*

Chile

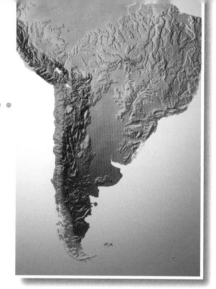

- **Capital:** Santiago. Area: 756,945 sq km. Currency: Chilean peso. Language: Spanish.

- **Physical features:** Highest mountain: Ojos del Salado (6908 m). Longest river: Bio-Bio (200 km).

- **Population:** 14.6 million. Population density: 19/sq km. Life expectancy: men 72.3 years; women 78.3 years.

- **Wealth:** GDP: $77 billion. GDP per head: $4820.

▲ *Chile is very long and narrow – 4,200 km long and less than 180 km wide.*

- **Exports:** Copper, iron, fresh fruit, wood pulp.

- **Chile** is one of the world's most volcanically active countries, with 75 active volcanoes. Chile also has eight of the world's highest active volcanoes, including Guallatir (6170 m) – the world's tallest.

- **Chile is a major** wine producer.

- **The copper mine** at Chuquicamata is the world's biggest man-made hole, four km long and 670 m deep. The El Teniente copper mine is the world's deepest.

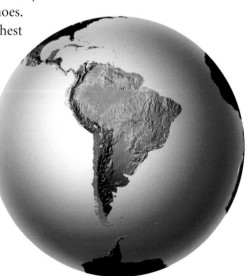

44

- **Chile** is the world's largest copper producer.
- **The Mapuche Indians** live in the forest area around Temuco in southern Chile and those who preserve their traditional way of life live in round straw houses.

▼ *Chile's spectacular landscape ranges from thick forests to huge glaciers, and from the Atacama desert to the Andes mountains. This impressive waterfall is found on the Bio Bio river.*

The Gran Chaco

- **The Gran Chaco** is a vast area of tropical grassland in Argentina, Paraguay and Bolivia.

- **It covers** an area of over 750 million sq km, an area as large as northwest Europe.

- **It is home** to scattered native Indian groups such as the Gaicurú, Lengua, Mataco, Vilela, Zamuco and Tupi people.

- **The word Chaco** comes from the Quechua Indian word for 'Hunting Land' because it is rich in wildlife. *Gran* is Spanish for 'big'.

- **The major activities** on the Chaco are cattle grazing and cotton growing.

- **In the east** huge factories have been built to process tannin from the trees for leather production.

- **In places** grass can grow up to 3 m tall, higher than a rider on horseback.

▶ *The maned wolf is found in the South American grasslands and scrub forest of Brazil, northern Argentina, Paraguay, and Bolivia.*

▲ *The jaguar is the Chaco's biggest hunting animal, and the biggest cat in the Americas. Yet unlike other big cats, it never roars. It just makes a strange cry rather like a loud sneeze.*

● **The Chaco** is home to many wild animals, including pumas, tapirs, giant rheas and giant armadillos.

● **The Chaco** is the last refuge of the South American maned or red wolf.

. . . FASCINATING FACT . . .
The sediments under the Gran Chaco
are well over 3000 m deep in places.

Argentina

- **Capital:** Buenos Aires. Area: 2,766,889 sq km. Currency: Peso. Language: Spanish.

- **Physical Features:** Highest mountain: Aconcagua (6960 m). Longest river: Paraná (3943 km).

- **Population:** 35.6 million. Population density: 13/sq km. Life expectancy: men 69.7 years; women 76.8 years.

- **Wealth:** GDP: $325 billion. GDP per head: $8950.

- **Exports:** Minerals, wheat, maize, meat, hides, wool, tannin, linseed oil, peanuts, processed foods.

- **The Argentinian landscape** is dominated by the pampas, the vast flat grasslands which stretch all the way to the high Andes mountains in the west.

◄ *Neighbourhoods called* barrios *occupy parts of Buenos Aires. These neighbourhoods are well-known for their brightly painted houses.*

- **Most of Argentina's** exports are pampas products – wheat, corn, meat, hides and wool.

- **Cattle** on the pampas – 50 million of them – are herded by Argentina's famous cowboys, the gauchos.

- **Argentina** is the most educated country in South America, with a third of students going to university.

... FASCINATING FACT ...
The region of Patagonia covers more than a quarter of Argentina but is home to less than 3% of the population.

▼ *The granite pinnacles of Fitzroy National Park include Mount Fitzroy and Cerro Torre, both of which reach heights of over 4000 m.*

Peoples of South America

- **South America** has a population of over 500 million people.

- **Before its conquest** by the Spanish and Portuguese in the 16th century, South America was home to many native peoples.

- **There are native villages** in the Andes with only one race, and a few native tribes in the Amazon rainforest who have had little contact with the outside world.

- **The main population groups now** are American Indians, whites, blacks (whose ancestors were brought as slaves) and people of mixed race.

- **Most people** in Latin America are mixed race.

- **The largest mixed race** groups are mestizos (people with both American Indian and white ancestors) and mulattoes (people with black and white ancestors).

- **Mestizos** are the majority in countries such as Paraguay and Venezuela. Mulattoes are the majority in Brazil.

- **The Europeans** who came to South America were mostly Spanish and Portuguese, so nearly two-thirds of South Americans speak Spanish.

- **Many American Indians** speak their own languages.

- **Quechua** is a native language, which Peru has made its official language along with Spanish.

▶ *In the Amazon, small tribes such as the Matses still survive as they have done for thousands of years.*

The United Kingdom

- **Capital:** London. Area: 242,534 sq km. Currency: Pound. Language: English.

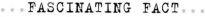
- **Physical features:** Highest mountain: Ben Nevis (1343 m). Longest river: the Severn (320 km).

- **Population:** 58.5 million. Population density: 239/sq km. Life expectancy: men 74.5 years; women 79.8 years.

- **Wealth:** GDP: $1231 billion. GDP per head: $20,870.

- **Exports:** Manufactured goods such as chemicals and electronics, meat and dairy products, whisky, financial services, music and publishing.

- **The British Isles** are 4000 islands with 20,000 km of coast. There are two large islands: Great Britain and Ireland. The United Kingdom (UK) is four countries joined politically – England, Scotland, Wales and N. Ireland.

- **England** is intensively farmed, especially in the south where wheat, barley, rape, sugar beet and vegetables are grown. In the moister west and north of England, especially, and Scotland and Wales, cattle and sheep are reared. The Welsh borders are famous for their orchards.

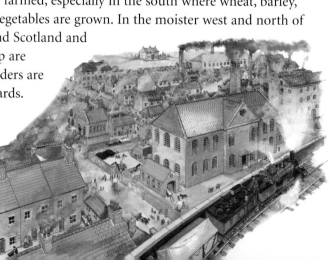

▶ *In the 1800s, northern coalfield cities were home to heavy industries such as steelmaking and engineering.*

52

▶ *England is the biggest and most densely populated of the countries of the UK. Wales is a land of hills and sheep farms, except for the south where industry is important. Much of Scotland is wild moors and valleys. A third of Northern Ireland's population lives in Belfast.*

- **The Industrial Revolution** began in the 1800s in cities such as Manchester and Leeds. Today, some northern towns are finding it difficult to survive, but southern England is thriving on light industries and services.

- **London** is one of the world's great financial centres. Over 500 international banks are crammed into a small area of the city called the Square Mile. Here billions of dollars' worth of money deals are done every day.

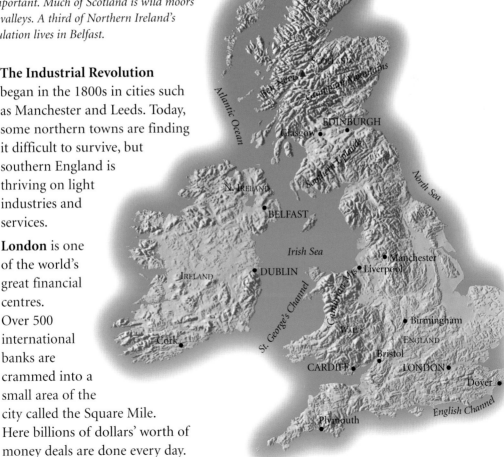

London

▲ *London's Houses of Parliament, and its tower with its bell Big Ben, were built in 1860 after a fire destroyed an earlier building.*

● **London** is the capital of the United Kingdom and is its largest city by far, with a population of about 7 million.

● **People have settled** here for thousands of years, but the city of London began with the Roman city of Londinium.

...**FASCINATING FACT**...
700,000 people work in banking and finance – more than in any other city in the world.

● **Throughout the 19th century** London was the world's biggest city, with a million people, and the hub of the world's largest empire, the British Empire.

- **London** is based on two ancient cities: the City of London, which developed from the Roman and Saxon towns, and Westminster, which developed around the palaces of English kings around 1000 years ago.

- **London** has 500,000 factory workers, but most people work in services, such as publishing and other media. London is one of the world's major finance centres.

- **Eight million tourists** come to London each year.

- **London's tallest building** is 244 m Canary Wharf Tower.

- **The London Eye** is the biggest wheel in the world, giving people a bird's eye view over London.

- **London's oldest large buildings** are the Tower of London and Westminster Abbey, both around 1000 years old. The Tower of London was built for William the Conqueror.

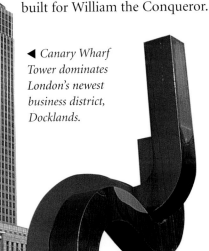

◀ *Canary Wharf Tower dominates London's newest business district, Docklands.*

▲ *The London Eye takes passengers on a 30 minute journey as high as 50 m above the Thames.*

55

Ireland

- **Capital (Eire):** Dublin. Area: 70,282 sq km. Currency: Punt. Languages: Irish and English. Over two-thirds of Ireland is in Eire, the Irish Republic. The rest is Northern Ireland or Ulster, which is part of the UK.

- **Physical features:** Highest mountain: Carrauntoohil (1041 m). Longest river: the Shannon (386 km).

- **Population (Eire):** 3.6 million. Population density: 51/sq km. Life expectancy: men 73.6 years; women 79.2 years.

- **Wealth (Eire):** GDP: $65.1 billion. GDP per head: $17,790.

- **Exports:** Livestock, dairy products, whiskey, machinery, chemicals, electronics.

- **Peat** is one of Ireland's few natural energy resources. Peat is the compressed rotten remains of plants found in peat bogs. Once dried it can be burned as fuel.

▲ *Blarney Castle, County Cork, is famous for the Blarney Stone, supposed to impart the gift of eloquence.*

- **Ireland** is still largely a poor farming country, famous for its pubs and folk music. But many young people are moving to the towns, or to other countries in search of work and a better lifestyle.

> ...**FASCINATING FACT**...
> Ireland breeds more winning racehorses than any comparable country in Europe.

- **Ireland,** and Dublin in particular, have begun to thrive in recent years – partly because of the success of high-tech electronics and computer industries.

- **Entertainment** is big business in Ireland. Many films – both American and Irish – are made in Ireland, and pop, rock and folk music are huge money earners.

▼ *Trinity College, Dublin, is the oldest university in Ireland, founded in 1592 by Queen Elizabeth 1 of England and Ireland.*

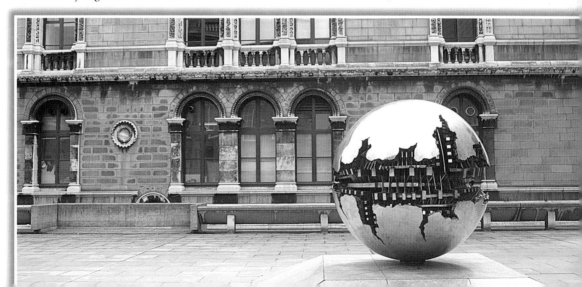

France

▲ *The Alpine peak Mont Blanc is on the France-Italy-Switzerland border.*

- **Capital:** Paris. Area: 543,965 sq km. Currency: Franc. Language: French.

- **Physical features:** Highest mountain: Mont Blanc (4807 m). Longest river: the Loire (1005 km).

- **Population:** 58.5 million. Population density: 105/sq km. Life expectancy: men 74.2 years; women 82 years.

- **Wealth:** GDP: $1542 billion. GDP per head: $26,300.

- **Exports:** Agricultural products, machinery, chemicals, food and wine.

- France is the biggest food producer in Europe, apart from Russia. In the north and west, wheat, sugar beet and many other crops are grown and dairy cattle are raised. In the warmer, drier south of France grapes and other fruit are grown.

- **France has limited** coal and oil reserves, but nuclear power gives France 75% of its energy.

- **France** is the biggest country in western Europe. Much is still rural, with ancient farmhouses and villages looking as if they have changed little in centuries. But French cities such as Lyons and Marseilles are famous for their sophisticated culture. They are also the centres of so much industry that France is the world's fourth largest industrial nation after the USA, Japan and Germany.

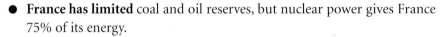

...**FASCINATING FACT**...
French vineyards produce more than a quarter of the world's wine every year.

● **The French** are famous for their *haute cuisine* (fine cooking). Later, plainer styles developed and a lighter style of cooking called *nouvelle cuisine* (new cooking) has developed to suit today's tastes.

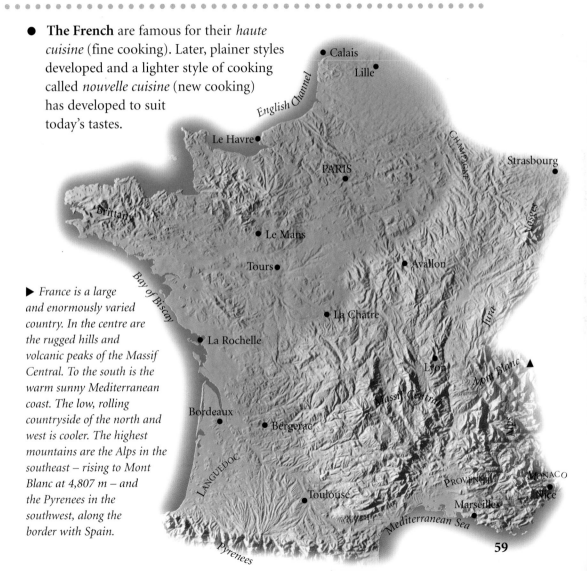

▶ *France is a large and enormously varied country. In the centre are the rugged hills and volcanic peaks of the Massif Central. To the south is the warm sunny Mediterranean coast. The low, rolling countryside of the north and west is cooler. The highest mountains are the Alps in the southeast – rising to Mont Blanc at 4,807 m – and the Pyrenees in the southwest, along the border with Spain.*

59

Paris

- **Paris** is the capital of France and its largest city with a population of just over two million.

- **Paris** is France's main business and financial centre. The Paris region is also a major manufacturing region, notably for cars.

- **Paris** is famed for luxuries such as perfume and fashion.

- **Paris** is known for restaurants such as La Marée, cafés such as Deux Magots and nightclubs such as the Moulin Rouge.

- **Paris** monuments include the Arc de Triomphe, the Eiffel Tower, Notre Dame cathedral and the Beauborg Centre.

◄ *The 300 m-high Eiffel Tower was built to celebrate the centenary of the French Revolution.*

▲ *Notre Dame is the most famous of the Gothic cathedrals of the Middle Ages and the setting for Victor Hugo's novel* Notre Dame de Paris.

- **Paris** gets its name from a Celtic tribe called the Parisii who lived there 2000 years ago.

- **The Roman general** Julius Caesar said the Parisii were 'clever, inventive and given to quarrelling among themselves'. Some say this is true of Parisians today.

- **Paris** was redeveloped in the 1850s and 60s by Baron Haussman on the orders of Emperor Napoleon III.

- **Haussman** gave Paris broad, tree-lined streets called boulevards, and grand, grey, seven-storey houses.

Netherlands and Belgium

- **Netherlands:** Capital: Amsterdam. Population: 15.6 million. Currency: Guilder. Language: Dutch.

- **Belgium:** Capital: Brussels. Population: 10.1 million. Currency: Belgian franc. Languages: Dutch, French and German.

- **Belgium and the Netherlands** are often called the Low Countries because they are both quite flat. The Netherlands' highest hill is just 321 m.

▶ *Holland is famous for its windmills. These are not for grinding flour but for working the pumps that keep the flat land dry.*

...**FASCINATING FACT**...
The Netherlands is the world's biggest trader in cut flowers.

- **A third of the Netherlands** (also known as Holland) is polders – land once covered by the sea, but now protected by banks called dykes and pumped dry.

- **The Netherlands** exports more cheese than any other country in the world. Edam and Gouda are famous.

- **The Netherlands** is famous for its vast fields of tulips.

- **Rotterdam** at the mouth of the Rhine is one of the world's biggest ports, handling a million tonnes of goods each day.

- **Brussels** is the seat of the European Union Commission and Council.

- **The Belgian** city of Antwerp is the diamond-cutting centre of the world.

▲ *Amsterdam is made up of more than 100 islands linked by canals.*

Netherlands

Belgium

63

Germany

- **Capital:** Berlin. Area: 357,868 sq km. Currency: Deutschemark. Language: German.

- **Physical features:** Highest mountain: Zugspitze (2963 m). Longest river: the Danube (2859 km).

- **Population:** 82.1 million. Population density: 229/sq km. Life expectancy: men 73.9 years; women 80.2 years.

- **Wealth:** GDP: $2321 billion. GDP per head: $28,280.

- **Exports:** Machinery, vehicles, chemicals, iron, steel, textiles, food, wine.

- **Germany** is the world's third biggest industrial nation after the USA and Japan, famous for its precision engineering and quality products, such as tools and machine tools.

▲ *Neuschwanstein, built for 'Mad' King Ludwig II of Bavaria in the 1870s, is the most famous of the many castles in Bavaria and Germany's Rhineland.*

- **Germany's smoky industrial** heartland was the Ruhr valley, where dozens of coalmines fed huge steelworks. Many mines and steelworks have now closed and many people have moved south to places such as Stuttgart and Munich to escape unemployment and dirty air. But the Ruhr remains important to industry.

- **Germany is** the world's third biggest car-maker after the USA and Japan. It is well-known for its upmarket cars such as Mercedes, BMW and Audi.

> ... **FASCINATING FACT** ...
> The reunification of Germany in 1990 made it western Europe's most populated country by far.

● **German farms** are often small, family-run affairs. Yet the country can grow almost all its own food – growing huge quantities of cereal and sugar beet, and raising large numbers of cows and pigs.

▶ *The flatter northern part of Germany is a mixture of heath, marsh and rich farmland, where cereals such as rye are widely grown. The south is mountainous, with powerful rivers flowing through deep, wooded valleys.*

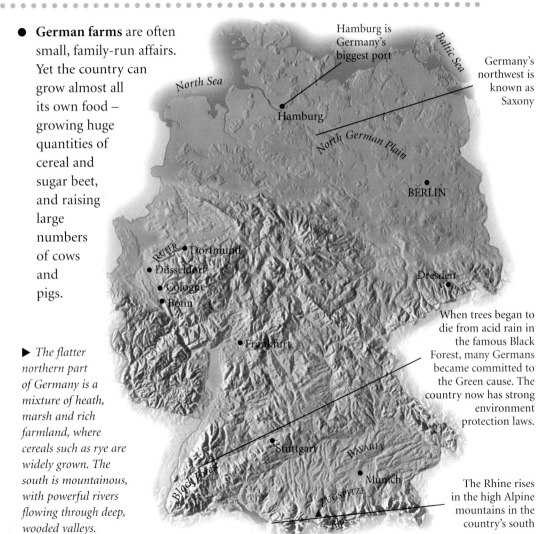

Hamburg is Germany's biggest port

Germany's northwest is known as Saxony

North Sea

Baltic Sea

Hamburg

North German Plain

BERLIN

RUHR • Dortmund
• Düsseldorf
• Cologne
• Bonn

Dresden

• Frankfurt

When trees began to die from acid rain in the famous Black Forest, many Germans became committed to the Green cause. The country now has strong environment protection laws.

Stuttgart

BAVARIA

Black Forest

• Munich

ZUGSPITZE

ALPS

The Rhine rises in the high Alpine mountains in the country's south

65

Berlin

- **Berlin** is Germany's capital and largest city, with a population of about 3.5 million.

- **Berlin** was originally capital of Prussia, which expanded to become Germany in the 1800s.

- **The city** was wrecked by Allied bombs in World War II.

- **After the War** Berlin was left inside the new communist East Germany and split into East and West by a high wall.

- **East Berlin** was the capital of East Germany; the West German capital moved to Bonn.

- **In 1989** the East German government collapsed and the Berlin Wall was torn down. East and West Germany were united in 1990 and Berlin was made capital again.

- **The Brandenburg Gate** is a huge stone arch built in 1791.

▶ *The Brandenburg Gate marked the boundary between East and West Berlin. In 1990 the east and west halves of the city were reunited.*

▲ *The Berlin Wall was built in 1961. Anyone caught trying to cross from the east to the west was killed.*

- **Kurfurstendamm** is a famous shopping avenue. The Hansa quarter was designed by architects in the 1950s.

- **Since reunification** many spectacular new buildings have been built in Berlin including the refurbished Reichstag designed by Norman Foster.

```
. . . FASCINATING FACT . . .
Almost every Berliner has a fragment of
the Wall, torn down in 1989.
```

67

Switzerland and Austria

Switzerland

Austria

- **Switzerland:** Capital: Berne. Population: 7.3 million. Currency: Franc. Languages: German, French and Italian.

- **Austria:** Capital: Vienna. Population: 8.1 million. Currency: Schilling. Language: German.

- **Switzerland and Austria** are small but beautiful countries mostly in the Alps mountains.

- **Both Switzerland and Austria** make a great deal of money from tourists who come to walk and ski here.

- **Switzerland** has long been 'neutral', staying out of all the major wars. This is why organizations such as the Red Cross and the World Health Organization are based there.

- **Switzerland is** the world's richest country in terms of GDP per person ($43,060).

- **People from** all over the world put their money in Swiss banks because the country is stable politically and its banking laws guarantee secrecy.

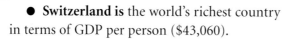

▶ *Austria earns more than a sixth of its income from tourists who come to enjoy the Alpine scenery.*

▲ *The enchanting Austrian city of Salzburg was the birthplace of Wolfgang Amadeus Mozart.*

- **Switzerland is famous** for making small, valuable things such as precision instruments and watches.
- **Vienna** was once the heart of the great Austrian Empire, and the music capital of Europe.
- **Austrians** rely on mountain-river hydroelectricity for much of their power.

The Alps

▲ *The pointed summit of the Matterhorn is the third highest peak of the Alps.*

- **The Alps** are Europe's largest mountain range, 1000 km long, up to 250 km wide and covering 210,000 sq km.

- **The highest Alpine peak** is Mont Blanc (4,807 m) on the France-Italy-Switzerland border.

- **Famous peaks** include the Matterhorn (4,478 m) and Monte Rosa (4807 m) on the Swiss-Italian border.

70

- **The Alps began to form** about 70 million years ago when the African crustal plate shifted into Europe.

- **The Alps are the source** of many of Europe's major rivers such as the Rhine, Rhone, Po and Danube.

- **Warm, dry, violent winds** called föhns blow down north facing slopes, melting snow and starting avalanches.

- **The high Alpine pastures** are famous for their summer grazing for dairy cows. In winter, the cows come down into the valleys. This is called transhumance.

- **The Alps** are being worn away by human activity. In valleys, cities and factories are growing, while skiing wears away the slopes at the tops of the mountains.

- **The Alps** have the world's highest vineyards, 1,500 m up.

▲ *Alpine cows are raised for their dairy produce rather than their meat.*

> **FASCINATING FACT**
> The highest village in the Swiss Alps is
> Chandolin which lies at a height of 2,000 m.

71

Scandinavia

- **Norway:** Capital: Oslo. Population: 4.4 million. Currency: Norwegian krone. Language: Norwegian.

- **Sweden:** Capital: Stockholm. Population: 8.9 million. Currency: Swedish krona. Language: Swedish.

▼ *Norway's mountainous coast has been gouged into deep fjords by glaciers.*

- **Denmark:** Capital: Copenhagen. Population: 5.3 million. Currency: Danish krone. Language: Danish.

- **Finland:** Capital: Helsinki. Population: 5.1 million. Currency: Markka. Languages: Finnish and Swedish.

- **Scandinavia** has some of the iciest, most northerly inhabited countries in the world. Yet they enjoy a high standard of living and welfare provision.

- **Norway's fishing boats** land 2.4 million tonnes of fish a year – more than those of any other European country except Russia.

- **Sweden is known** for its high-quality engineering, including its cars such as Volvos, and for its aircraft-makers such as Saab.

- **Finland and Sweden** are known for their glass and ceramic work.

- **Sweden's capital Stockholm** is built on four islands in an archipelago of 24,000 islands.

- **Danish farms** are famous for butter and bacon.

North European food

- **Fish and bread** play a major role in the traditional Scandinavian diet.

- **Gravadlax** is a Swedish form of smoked salmon, usually served with pepper, dill and mustard sauce.

- **Smörgåsbord** is a Swedish speciality. It is a huge spread of bread and cold foods, including fish such as herring and salmon, and also cheeses.

- **Smörgåsbord** gets its name from the Swedish smörgås, meaning bread, and bord, meaning table.

- **Every region in Germany** has its own range of produce, but foods such as wurst (sausages), pretzels and sauerkraut (pickled cabbage) are widely popular.

▶ *Traditionally, smoking fish such as salmon was a way of preserving it. Today, people still enjoy its unique flavour.*

▲ *In the UK roast beef is served with traditional Yorkshire pudding, made from a batter of flour, eggs and milk.*

- **The German national drink** is beer, and every October a huge beer festival is held in Munich.

- **England is well known** for its hearty stews and winter roasts, especially roast beef. But the most popular food for those eating out is Indian.

- **An English speciality** is fish (deep-fried in batter) and chips (fried slices of potato).

- **Vienna** in Austria is renowned for its coffee houses where the Viennese sit and eat Kaffee und Kuchen (coffee and cakes).

- **Poland is famous** for its rye bread and thick beet.

▲ *Lager, a type of beer, is popular in northern Europe.*

Peoples of Europe

- **About 700 million** people live in Europe – about 12% of the world's population.

  - **Europe** is one of the most densely populated continents, averaging 67 people per square kilometre.

  - **Most Europeans** are descended from tribes who migrated into Europe more than 1500 years ago.

  - **Most British people** are descended from a mix of Celts, Angles, Saxons, Danes and others. Most French people are descended from Gauls and Franks. Most Eastern Europeans are Slavic (see peoples of Northern Asia).

  - **Northern Europeans** such as Scandinavians often have fair skin and blonde hair. Southern Europeans such as Italians often have olive skin and dark hair.

  - **Most European countries** have a mix of people from all parts of the world, including former European colonies in Africa and Asia.

◀ *In Eastern Europe, many people, like this Romanian, have their own traditional dress.*

- **Most Europeans** are Christians.

- **Most Europeans** speak an Indo-European language, such as English, French or Russian.

- **Languages** such as French, Spanish and Italian are romance languages that come from Latin, language of the Romans.

- **Basque people** in Spain speak a language related to no other language. Hungarians, Finns and Estonians speak a Uralic-Altaic language like those of Turkey and Mongolia.

▶ *Traditional lace caps and full skirts are still worn in a few regions of the Netherlands, including the islands of Zeeland.*

Russia

- **Capital:** Moscow. Area: 17,075,400 sq km. Currency: Rouble. Language: Russian.
- **Physical features:** Highest mountain: Mt Elbrus (5642 m). Longest river: the Ob-Irtysh (5411 km).
- **Population:** 147.7 million. Population density: 9/sq km. Life expectancy: men 60.6 years; women 72.8 years.
- **Wealth:** GDP: $394.9 billion. GDP per head: $2680. Exports: chemicals, machinery, minerals, natural gas, paper products, petroleum, wood products.
- **Russia** or the Russian Federation is the country created by the Russians after the break up of the Soviet Union in 1991. It includes republics such as Chechnya, Osetiya, Kalmykiya, Tatarstan, Mordoviya and Bashkortostan. Many of these republics, such as Chechnya, are waiting to be independent.
- **Russia is** the biggest country in the world, almost twice as big as the next country, Canada. It stretches from the subtropical south to the Arctic north, where it has the longest Arctic coastline of any country.
- **Russia has huge** mineral resources and is among the world's leading producers of oil, natural gas, coal, asbestos, manganese, silver, tin and zinc. It also has giant forests for timber in the east in Siberia.

▲ *Lake Baikal in Siberia, Russia, contains about one-fifth of all the world's fresh water. The water is carried there by 336 rivers that flow into it. Lake Baikal has the world's only freshwater seals, and among its many unique animals is a fish that bears live young.*

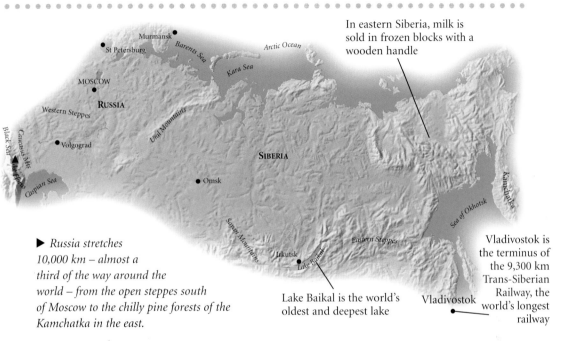

In eastern Siberia, milk is sold in frozen blocks with a wooden handle

▶ *Russia stretches 10,000 km – almost a third of the way around the world – from the open steppes south of Moscow to the chilly pine forests of the Kamchatka in the east.*

Lake Baikal is the world's oldest and deepest lake

Vladivostok is the terminus of the 9,300 km Trans-Siberian Railway, the world's longest railway

- **Russia** has some of the biggest factories in the world around Moscow. Yet in the far north and east, people still live simply, herding reindeer or hunting.

- **After the USSR broke up,** Russia and its people were plunged into crisis. Encouraged by western nations, Russian presidents – first Boris Yeltsin, then Vladimir Putin – have tried to establish a free market economy in place of the old communist one.

. . . **FASCINATING FACT** . . .
In Yakutsk in Siberia, winter temperatures can plunge to -69°C while summers can soar to 39°C – more extreme than anywhere else. Oymako is the world's coldest town. It once had temperatures of -72°C.

The Russian steppes

- **The steppes** are a vast expanse of temperate grassland, stretching right across Asia.

- **'Steppes'** is the Russian word for grassland.

- **The Western Steppe** extends 4000 km from the grassy plains of the Ukraine through Russia and Kazakhstan to the Altai mountains on the Mongolian border.

- **The steppes** extend 300-800 km from north to south.

- **The Eastern Steppe** extends 2500 km from the Altai across Mongoliato Manchuria in north China.

- **The Eastern Steppe** is higher and colder than the Western Steppe and the difference between winter and summer is as extreme as anywhere on Earth.

- **Nomadic herders** have lived on the steppes for over 6000 years.

- **It was on the steppes** near the Black and Caspian Seas that people probably first rode horses 5000 years ago.

- **The openness** of the steppes meant that travel by horse was easy long before roads were built.

▶ *Nomadic herders and their camels make their way across the steppes. Their way of life is slowly dying out.*

···**FASCINATING FACT**···
The steppes extend 8,000 km across
Eurasia, a fifth of the way round the world.

Moscow and St Petersburg

- **Moscow** is the largest city in the Russian Federation and is capital of Russia.

- **Moscow** is Russia's main industrial centre, with huge textile and car-making plants, such as the Likhachyov works.

- **Moscow's biggest shops** are Detsky Mir (Children's World) and GUM, the government store on Red Square.

- **Moscow's historic centre** is Red Square and the Kremlin, the walled city-within-a-city.

- **In the past** Moscow had wooden buildings and was often burnt down, most famously by Napoleon's troops in 1812.

- **Moscow is snow-covered** from November to April each year, but snow-ploughs keep all the main roads clear.

- **St Petersburg** is Russia's second largest city.

▶ *The Cathedral of St Basil is in Red Square and is made up of eight chapels, each one capped by a unique onion dome.*

▲ *St Petersburg is an elegant city with many beautiful houses and palaces such as the famous Hermitage museum.*

● **St Petersburg** was founded in 1703 by Tsar Peter the Great to be his capital instead of Moscow.

● **After the 1917 Russian Revolution,** communists called Petersburg (then called Petrograd) Leningrad and made Moscow capital. St Petersburg regained its name in 1991.

> ...**FASCINATING FACT**...
> Leningrad was dubbed 'Hero City' for its desperate defence against the Nazis from 1941-44.

Poland and neighbours

- **Poland:** Capital: Warsaw. Population: 38.7 million. Currency: Zloty. Language: Polish.

- **Lithuania:** Capital: Vilnius. Population: 3.7 million. Currency: Litas. Language: Lithuanian.

- **Latvia:** Capital: Riga. Population: 2.5 million. Currency: Lats. Language: Latvian.

- **Estonia:** Capital: Tallinn. Population: 1.4 million. Currency: Kroon. Language: Estonian.

- **Poland** was led away from communism by trade union leader Lech Walesa, who became the first president of democratic Poland in 1990.

- **The name Poland** comes from the Slavic word *polane* which means plain, and much of Poland is flat plains.

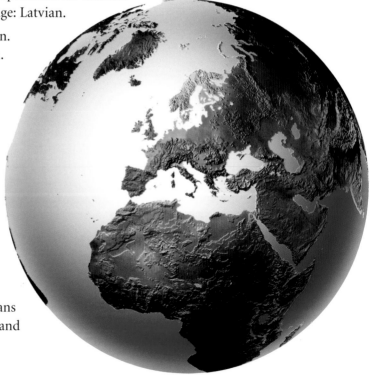

- **The shipyards at Gdansk** on the Baltic make Poland the world's fifth largest builder of merchant ships.

- **Krakow** has many historic buildings but the nearby Nowa Huta steelworks make it very polluted.

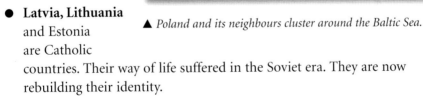

▲ *Poland and its neighbours cluster around the Baltic Sea.*

- **Latvia, Lithuania** and Estonia are Catholic countries. Their way of life suffered in the Soviet era. They are now rebuilding their identity.

- **Latvian** is one of the oldest European languages, related to the ancient Indian language Sanskrit.

Poland

Latvia

Lithuania

Estonia

85

Ukraine and Belarus

- **Ukraine:** Capital: Kiev. Population: 51.3 million. Currency: Hryvnya. Language: Ukrainian.

- **Belarus:** Capital: Minsk. Population: 10.4 million. Currency: Belarusian rouble. Language: Belarussian.

- **Ukraine** is Europe's largest country (except for Russia), covering over 600,000 sq km.

- **Ukraine** is famous for its vast plains or steppes. The fertile black soils have made it 'the breadbasket of Europe', growing huge amounts of wheat and barley.

- **During the Soviet era** Soviet policies forced Ukrainians to speak Russian and adopt Russian culture, but the Ukrainian identity has been found again since they gained independence in 1991.

▲ *Ukraine and Belarus are flat countries that form the western margin of Russia, north of the Black Sea.*

- **In the Soviet era** over a quarter of Ukraine's industrial output was arms. Now Ukraine is trying to use these factories to make other products.

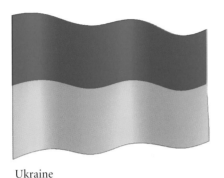

Ukraine

Belarus

- **In 1986** a terrible accident occurred at the Chernobyl nuclear power plant north of Kiev. A reactor exploded spreading radioactivity over a wide area.

- **Nuclear energy** still provides 25% of Ukraine's power, but many Ukrainians are firmly against it.

- **Belarus** (known as Byelorussia under the USSR) is a flat country, covered in many places by thick forests and marshes. The Pripet Marshes are the largest in Europe covering 27,000 sq km.

- **Belarus** is known for making heavy-duty trucks, tractors and bicycles among other things. The forests provide products such as furniture, matches and paper.

Hungary and neighbours

- **Hungary:** Capital: Budapest. Population: 10.3 million. Currency: Forint. Language: Hungarian.

- **Czech Republic:** Capital: Prague. Population: 10.3 million. Currency: Koruna. Language: Czech.

- **Slovakia:** Capital: Bratislava. Population: 5.4 million. Currency: Koruna. Language: Slovak.

- **Slovenia:** Capital: Ljubljana. Population: 1.9 million. Currency: Tolar. Language: Slovenian.

- **Until 1990** all of these countries were under Soviet rule, but they are all now democratic republics.

- **Since 1990,** the historic city of Prague has become a popular destination, especially with the young, and many recording artists have worked in studios here.

- **The Czech Republic** is famous for Pilsener beer brewed in the town of Pilsen with hops grown locally.

◀ *Hungary is one of the world's leading producers of sunflower oil, and in summer vast areas of its Great Plain turn yellow with sunflower blooms.*

▲ *Prague is one of the oldest and most beautiful cities in central Europe. It lies on the Vltava river and is known as the city of spires because of its many churches.*

- **Hungary's** national dish is goulash. This is a rich stew made from meat, onion and potatoes, spiced with paprika (red pepper) and served with black rye bread.

- **Slovakian people** were largely rural until recently, with a strong tradition of folk music, dancing and dress. Now many people are moving into industrial towns.

- **Vienna's white** Lippizaner horses are bred in Slovenia.

89

Romania and Bulgaria

- **Romania:** Capital: Bucharest. Population: 22.6 million. Currency: Leu. Language: Romanian.

- **Bulgaria:** Capital: Sofia. Population: 8.4 million. Currency: Lev. Language: Bulgarian.

- **Romania** gets its name from the Romans who occupied it almost 2000 years ago.

- **Transylvania** is a beautiful, wooded, mountain area of Romania, once home to the 15th-century tyrant Vlad the Impaler, the original Dracula.

- **Like Bulgaria,** Romania was communist until 1989 when the people overthrew President Ceausescu.

- **Ceausescu's** attempts to develop industry forced people off the lands into towns. Many orphans were left as families broke up.

- **Romania** is a major wine grower.

Romania   Bulgaria

- **Romania** is home not only to native Romanians but 250,000 Romanies (gypsies) who often live in caravans.

- **The Valley of Roses** is a valley near Kazanluk in Bulgaria full of fields of damask roses.

- **Bulgarian women pick** damask rose blossoms to get the oil to make 'attar of roses', used for perfumes.

▶ *The Dracula of legend really existed as prince Vlad Tepes II. His castle was in Tirgoviste, Transylvania.*

91

Spain and Portugal

▲ *Produce such as olives, oranges and grapes are grown in the central area of Spain. Olives are a successful Spanish export product, with Spain ranking as one of the leading olive-growing countries.*

- **Spain:** Capital: Madrid. Area: 504,782 sq km. Currency: Peseta. Language: Spanish.

- **Physical features:** Highest mountain: Mulhacén (3478 m). Longest river: Tagus (1007 km).

- **Population:** 39.6 million. Population density: 78/sq km. Life expectancy: men 74.5 years; women 81.5 years.

- **Wealth:** GDP: $569.6 billion. GDP per head: $14,490.

- **Exports:** Cars, wine, machinery, fruit, olive oil, steel, textiles, chemicals.

- **Much of the centre of Spain** is too hot and dry for some crops, but perfect for olives, sunflowers and for grapes, oranges and other fruit. Spain is one of the world's leading fruit-growers.

> ...**FASCINATING FACT**...
> Every summer, 55 million sunseekers come to the beaches of Spain's Costa del Sol.

Portugal

- **Spain is one of the foremost** car makers in Europe, with huge plants in Valencia and Saragossa. It also makes a lot of iron and steel. Toledo in the south was once famous for its fine sword steel.

Spain

- **Portugal:** Capital: Lisbon. Population: 9.9 million. Currency: Escudo. Language: Portuguese.

- **Portugal** once had a big empire including large parts of Latin America and Africa. Yet it is fairly underdeveloped. Most people still live in the countryside, growing wheat, rice, almonds, olives and maize. Portugal is famous for its 'port', a drink made by adding brandy to wine.

Italy

- **Capital:** Rome. Area 301,245 sq km. Currency: Lira. Language: Italian.

- **Physical features:** Highest mountain: Monte Rosa (4638 m). Longest river: Po (652 km).

- **Population:** 57.4 million. Population density: 190/sq km. Life expectancy: men 75 years; women 81.2.

- **Wealth:** GDP: $1,160 billion. GDP per head: $20,100.

- **Exports:** Wine, machinery, cars and trucks, footwear, clothes, olive oil, textiles, mineral products.

- **Italy** is a narrow, mountainous country. The north is cool and moist, with big industrial cities. Tuscany and Umbria have rich farmland and ancient cities famous for their art treasures. The south is hot, dusty and often poor.

- **Vines and olives** are grown widely and Italy is one of the world's main producers of both wine and olive oil.

- **Italy is one of the biggest** industrial nations. Industry is concentrated in the north in cities such as Turin and Milan. Here they make cars, computers, chemicals and textiles.

▲ *The Tuscan landscape has changed little from that depicted by Renaissance artists.*

- **Italians** like to dress in style and the fashion trade is big business. Italian fashion labels such as Armani, Versace, Valentino, Moschino and Gucci are now world famous.

- **Italy is full of beautiful** historic towns such as Florence, Padua and Mantua, many dating from the Renaissance.

▼ *The ancient city of Venice is set on 117 islands in a lagoon. Instead of streets, there are 177 canals, plied by boats called gondolas.*

Rome

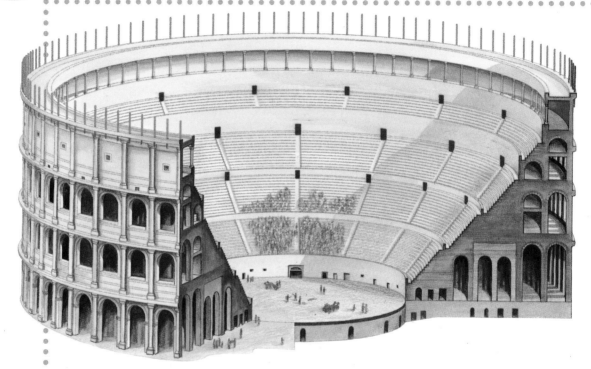

▲ *Arenas such as the Colosseum in Rome were built for games where gladiators fought to the death. Up to 80,000 people would have watched these spectacles.*

- **Rome** is the capital of Italy, and its biggest city, with a population of almost three million.
- **Rome's Vatican** is the home of the Pope.
- The Vatican is the smallest independent country in the world covering just 0.4 sq km.

- **Rome is known** as the eternal city because of its long and dramatic history.

- **Ancient Rome ruled** much of Europe and the lands around the Mediterranean for hundreds of years as the capital of the Roman Empire.

- **Ancient Rome** was famously built on seven hills – the Aventine, Caelian, Capitoline, Esquiline, Palatine, Quirinal and Viminal.

- **Rome has** one of the richest collections of art treasures and historic buildings in the world. The Trevi is one of many beautiful fountains.

- **There are many ancient Roman** relics in Rome including the Colosseum arena and the Pantheon.

- **The Vatican's** Sistine Chapel has a ceiling painted brilliantly by Michelangelo and frescoes (wall paintings) by Botticelli, Ghirlandaio and Perugino.

- **Rome is** now a major centre for film-making, publishing and tourism.

▲ *St Peter's Church is located in the Vatican city in Rome. It is the largest church in the world.*

97

Greece

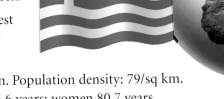

- **Capital:** Athens. Area: 131,957 sq km. Currency: Drachma. Language: Greek.

- **Physical features:** Highest mountain: Mt Olympus (2917 m).

- **Population:** 10.6 million. Population density: 79/sq km. Life expectancy: men 75.6 years; women 80.7 years.

- **Wealth:** GDP: $122.4 billion. GDP per head: $11,640.

- **Exports:** Clothes, olive oil, marble, petroleum products, fruit and tobacco.

▲ *Athena was the guardian goddess of Athens. She was honoured in the Parthenon by this 18 m high statue of ivory and gold.*

- **Farming:** Greece is so mountainous that only a third can be farmed, but a third of all workers work on the land, many raising goats or growing olives or vines for wine.

- **Greece** is the world's third largest grower of olives after Spain and Italy.

- **Greek salad** includes olives and feta cheese from goats milk. In some small villages, bakers allow villagers to cook their food in their *fuorno* oven.

- **More than ten million** visitors come to Greece each year – some to see the relics of Ancient Greece, but most to soak up the sun.

- **Athens** is the ancient capital of Greece, dominated by the Acropolis with its famous Parthenon temple ruins. Athens is also a modern city, with pollution caused by heavy traffic.

▲ *Greece is one of the most mountainous countries in Europe.*

99

Mediterranean food

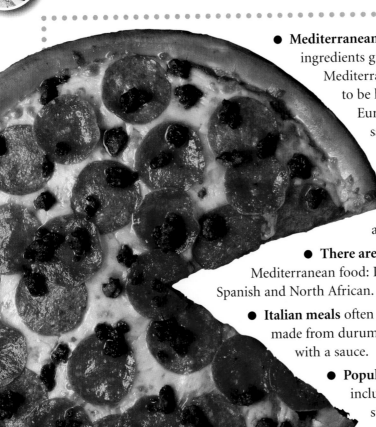

- **Mediterranean food** depends on ingredients grown in the warm Mediterranean climate. It tends to be lighter than north European food, including salads, flat bread and fish rather than sauces and stews.

- **Olive oil** is used for dressing salads and frying food.

- **There are five major styles** of Mediterranean food: Italian, Greek, Turkish, Spanish and North African.

- **Italian meals** often include pasta, which is made from durum wheat flour and served with a sauce.

- **Popular forms of pasta** include spaghetti ('little strings'), vermicelli ('little worms'), fusilli ('spindles') and tube-shaped macaroni.

◀ *Pizzas originated in Italy. They are made from a dough base spread with toppings such as tomatoes, cheese, olives and salami.*

- **In north Italy** ribbon pastas served with cream sauces are popular. In the south, macaroni served with tomato-based sauces are a more common dish.

- **Pizzas** are a favourite snack, especially in the south.

- **Greek food** includes meats – especially lamb – and fish cooked in olive oil.

- **Greek salad** includes olives, cucumber, tomatoes, herbs and feta cheese (soft goat's cheese).

- **Spanish food** often includes seafood such as calamares (squid). Paella includes seafoods and chicken combined with rice and cooked in saffron. Gazpacho is a cold tomato soup. Tapas are small snacks, originating in northern Spain.

▲ *Spaghetti Bolognese – spaghetti pasta with meat and tomato sauce – is the centrepiece of a typical Italian meal.*

101

Balkan peninsula

- **The Balkan peninsula** is a mountainous region in Southeast Europe between the Adriatic and Aegean Seas.

- **The Balkans** include many different nations, which were under either the Austro-Hungarian or Turkish Empires until 1918.

- **From 1918 to 1991** Serbia, Croatia, Bosnia and Herzegovina, Macedonia, Slovenia, Montenegro and Kosovo were joined as communist Yugoslavia.

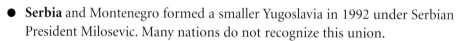

- **Bosnia** Herzegovina, Croatia, Macedonia, Slovenia and Kosovo broke away from Yugoslavia in the 1990s amid much bitter conflict.

- **Serbia** and Montenegro formed a smaller Yugoslavia in 1992 under Serbian President Milosevic. Many nations do not recognize this union.

- **Yugoslavia:** Capital: Belgrade. Population: 10.6 million. Currency: Dinar. Language: Serbo-croatian.

- **Croatia:** Capital: Zagreb. Population: 4.8 million. Currency: Kuna. Language: Serbo-croatian.

- **Bosnia:** Capital: Sarajevo. Population: 3.5 million. Currency: Bosnian dinar. Language: Serbo-croatian.

- **Albania:** Capital: Tirana. Population: 3.4 million. Currency: New lek. Language: Albanian.

- **Macedonia:** Capital: Skopje. Population: 2.3 m. Currency: Denar. Language: Macedonian.

▼ *The influence of the Roman Empire in Croatia can be been in this ancient Roman amphitheatre.*

Turkey and Cyprus

Turkey   Cyprus

- **Turkey:** Capital: Ankara. Population: 63.4 million. Currency: Turkish Lira. Language: Turkish.

- **Cyprus:** Capital: Nicosia. Population: 708,000. Currency: Cyprus pound. Languages: Greek and Turkish.

- **Turkey lies** partly in Europe, partly in Asia. The two continents are separated by a narrow sea called the Bosphorus.

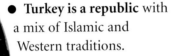

- **Turkey is a republic** with a mix of Islamic and Western traditions.

- **Istanbul** is one of the world's great historic capital cities. As Byzantium, it was capital of the Byzantine Empire for 1000 years. Then it was Constantinople, the capital of the great Ottoman Empire for 500 years, until 1920.

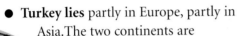

- **Street cafés** are popular with Turkish men, who come to drink thick, dark, sweet Turkish coffee, smoke pipes called hubble-bubbles and play backgammon.

▲ *Cyprus is famous for its hilltop castles, historic churches and mountain scenery.*

- **25 million Kurds** live on the borders of Turkey, Iran, Iraq and Syria and have no country of their own.

- **31% of Turkish people** live in the country growing wheat, cotton, tobacco, sugar beet, fruit and tea.

- **Turkey's national motto** is *Yurtta sulh, Cihand sulh* ('Peace at home, peace in the world').

- **Turkish food** is famous for its shish kebabs – cubes of meat and vegetables barbecued on a skewer.

▶ *Istanbul is the largest city and seaport of Turkey. It is unique because it is located on two continents – Asia and Europe!*

Georgia and neighbours

▶ *Tbilisi lies on the banks of the Kur River. The city is a combination of new and old with some buildings dating back centuries.*

- **Georgia:** Capital: Tbilisi. Population: 5.4 million. Currency: Lari. Language: Georgian.

- **Armenia:** Capital: Yerevan. Population: 3.8 million. Currency: Dram. Language: Armenian.

- **Azerbaijan:** Capital: Baku. Population: 7.7 million. Currency: Manat. Language: Azeri.

- **Georgia, Azerbaijan and Armenia** were once part of the Soviet Union.

- **In Georgia more people** live to be 100 years old than anywhere else in the world.

- **Georgia's capital Tbilisi** is said to be one of the world's oldest cities.

- **The oil** under the Caspian Sea off Azerbaijan once helped the Soviet Union produce half the world's oil. Villages on floating platforms house oilworkers.

- **New oil** strikes suggest there are 200 billion barrels of oil under the Caspian Sea – as much as in Iran and Iraq combined.

- **Oil has made** some people around the Caspian Sea rich, while others have remained desperately poor.

- **America, Russia** and other countries are locked in dispute over the route for oil pipelines from the Caspian Sea.

▼ *Armenia was the first country in the world to make Christianity its official religion.*

Peoples of northern Asia

- **83% of Russians** are descended from a group of people called Slavs who first lived in eastern Europe 5000 years ago.

- **East Slavs** are the Great Russians (or Russians), the Ukrainians and the Belorussians (or White Russians).

- **West Slavs** are eastern Europeans such as Czechs, Poles and Slovaks.

- **South Slavs** are Balkan people such as Croats, Serbs and Slovenes.

- **Slavs speak** Slavic or Slavonic languages such as Russian, Polish or Czech.

- **In the old Soviet Union** there were over 100 ethnic groups. 70% were Slavs. Many of the rest were Turkic people such as Uzbeks, Kazakhs and Turkmen. Many of these peoples now have their own nations.

▲ *Mongol warriors wore helmets of iron or hard leather and armour made from iron plates.*

▶ *Mongolian nomads live on the grassland steppes of central Asia, where they raise herds of goats, cattle and yaks. These nomads live in tents called yurts, which are traditionally covered with felt.*

- **Slavic** people are mainly Christian; Turkic people are mainly Islamic.

- **Many Turkic peoples** such as the Kazakhs have a nomadic tradition that is fast vanishing.

- **The Mongols** were a people whose empire under the great Khans once spread far south into China and far west across Asia.

- **The Tatars** are six million Turkic people who now live mainly in the Tatar Republic in the Russian Federation.

Kazakhstan and neighbours

- **Kazakhstan:** Capital: Akmola. Population: 16.37 million. Currency: Tenge. Language: Kazakh.

- **Uzbekistan:** Capital: Tashkent. Population: 24.1 million. Currency: Som. Language: Uzbek.

- **Turkmenistan:** Capital: Ashkabad. Population: 4.7 million. Currency: Manat. Language: Turkmen.

- **Many of the people** in this part of the world are still nomads, moving from place to place in search of new pastures for their herds.

- **Uzbekistan** has become wealthy from natural gas and also from cotton, which they call 'white gold'.

- **The Baykonur Cosmodrome** in Kazakhstan is where the Russians launch most of their spacecraft.

Kazakhstan

Uzbekistan

Turkmenistan

- **The Soviet Union** forced nomads in Kalmykiya by the Caspian Sea to boost sheep production beyond what the fragile steppe grass could handle. This created 1.4 million acres of desert.

- **The Aral Sea** on the Kazakh/Uzbek border was once the world's fourth largest lake. But irrigating farmland has cut the supply of water from the Amu Darya River and the Aral Sea is now shrinking rapidly.

- **The Caspian Sea** once had the sturgeon fish giving the most highly prized beluga caviar, but pollution has decimated the fish population.

▶ *The Russian sturgeon is so valuable that some fish farms employ armed guards to protect against thieves.*

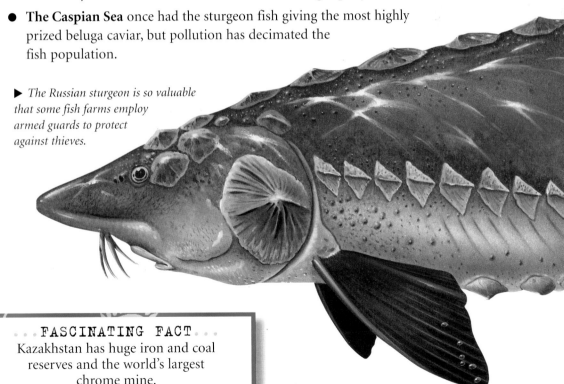

.... FASCINATING FACT ....
Kazakhstan has huge iron and coal
reserves and the world's largest
chrome mine.

111

The Near East

- **Syria:** Capital: Damascus. Population: 14.9 million. Currency: Syrian pound. Language: Arabic.

- **Jordan:** Capital: Amman. Population: 6.1 million. Currency: Jordan dinar. Language: Arabic.

- **The Lebanon:** Capital: Beirut. Population: 3.1 million. Currency: Lebanese pound. Language: Arabic.

- **Damascus** was a major trading centre 4000 years ago.

- **Syria** is at the western end of the belt of rich farmland known as the fertile crescent, which was the cradle of the earliest civilizations, along the banks of the Tigris and Euphrates rivers.

- **Most Syrian farmers** still work on small plots growing cotton and wheat. Today, however, 40% of Syrians now work in services.

- **Around 70% of Jordan's** income is from services such as tourism and banking.

- **The people of Syria,** Jordan and Lebanon are mostly Arabs. 90% of Syrians and Jordanians are Muslims, but 40% of Lebanese are Christians.

▲ *With the Euphrates being the home of the world's first civilisation, history is still ever-present. This Roman bridge, built in the 2nd century* AD, *is used even today.*

● **In 1948** Palestine was split between Israel, Jordan and Egypt. Palestinian Arabs' desire for their own country has caused conflict with Israelis.

● **In 1996** Israeli troops withdrew from the Gaza strip region, and Palestinians elected their own local administration.

113

Israel

- **Capital:** Jerusalem. Area: 20,770 sq km. Currency: New Shekel. Languages: Hebrew, Arabic.

- **Physical features:** Highest mountain: Mt Meron (1208 m). Longest river: River Jordan (359 km).

- **Population:** 5.9 million. Population density: 264/sq km. Life expectancy: men 75.7 years; women 79.7 years.

- **Wealth:** GDP: $94.4 billion. GDP per head: $16,180.

- **Exports:** Fruit and vegetables, chemical products, oil products, diamonds, textiles, machinery, fertilizers.

- **Israel** was founded in 1948 as a home for Jews who have since come here from all over the world.

- **The city of Jericho** may be the oldest in the world, dating back more than 10,000 years.

> **FASCINATING FACT**
> Jerusalem is sacred for three major religions: Judaism, Islam and Christianity.

- **Many people** in rural areas work on kibbutzim – collective farms where work and profits are shared.
- **Israel is famous** for its Jaffa oranges, named after Jaffa, the old name for the city of Tel Aviv. They are grown on the Plain of Sharon.

▼ *Many of the houses in Israel have flat roofs. They are surrounded by low walls to stop inhabitants from falling over the edges.*

115

Iraq and Iran

- **Iran:** Capital: Tehran. Population: 64.6 million. Currency: Iranian rial. Language: Persian (Farsi).

  - **Iraq:** Capital: Baghdad. Population: 21.2 million. Currency: Iraqi dinar. Language: Arabic.

    - **Iran is the largest** non-Arabic country in the Middle East. Iranians are descended from Persians.

    - **Iran was once** called Persia, and was the centre of an empire ruled by the Shah that dates back thousands of years. The last Shah was overthrown in 1979.

    - **Iran is an Islamic** country, and the strong views of religious leader Ayatollah Khomeini (who died in 1989) played a key role in the revolution in 1979, which brought him to power.

- **Iran is famous for its carpets,** often called Persian carpets. They are Iran's second largest export, after oil. Oil brings Iran 80% of its export earnings.

Iraq

- **Iraq** was the place where civilization probably began 7000 years ago. The Greeks called it Mesopotamia.

- **Since 1979** Iraq has been ruled by Saddam Hussein and his leadership has brought the country into conflict with much of the world – especially when he invaded Kuwait. This started the Gulf War in 1991 when the USA and other nations retaliated.

Iran

- **Only about** a sixth of Iraq is suitable for farming and so it has to import much of its food, but it is one of the world's major oil producers.

- **United Nations** sanctions applied after the Gulf War still restrict trade with Iraq. Some argue that it is poor Iraqis who suffer from these and not Saddam Hussein.

▼ *Gas released while drilling for oil in Iraq is burnt off, producing vast flames.*

The Middle East

- **Saudi Arabia:** Capital: Riyadh.
  Population: 19.5 million.
  Currency: Riyal.
  Language: Arabic.

- **Yemen:** Capital: San'a.
  Population: 16.3 million.
  Currencies: Yemeni dinar, riyal.
  Language: Arabic.

- **Kuwait:** Capital: Kuwait City.
  Population: 1.7 m. Currency:
  Kuwaiti dinar. Language: Arabic.

- **United Arab Emirates (UAE):**
  Capital: Abu Dhabi.
  Population: 2.3 million.
  Currency: Dirham.
  Language: Arabic.

- **Population:** Oman: 2.3
  million. Bahrain: 600,000.

▶ *The Dar Al Hajjar
(Palace of the Rock),
Yemen is perched on the
top of a rocky pinnacle
near San'a.*

Qatar: 600,000.

- **Much of the Middle East** is desert. Rub'al Khali in Saudi lives up to its name, Empty Quarter. Tent-dwelling nomads called Bedouins have herded sheep and goats here for thousands of years. Now most Bedouins live in houses.

- **Oil has made** the Arab states rich. People in the UAE, Bahrain and Kuwait have a higher income per head than any country outside Europe.

- **Saudi Arabia** is the world's leading exporter of oil and second only to Russia as oil producer. It has 25% of the world's known oil reserves.

- **Yemen** is one of the world's poorest countries.

- **The oil-rich states** along the Gulf are short of water. Most comes from wells, but now they are building desalination plants which remove salt so they can use water from the sea.

▲ *Civilization began in the Middle East, but the climate dried and turned much of it to desert.*

Peoples of the Middle East

- **People have farmed** in the Middle East longer than anywhere else in the world.

- **The Middle East** was the site of the first cities and ancient civilizations such as those of Sumer and Babylon.

- **Most people** in the Middle East are Arabs.

- **Arabic is spoken** in all Middle East countries except for Iran where Farsi (Persian) is spoken, Turkey where most speak Turkish, and Israel where most speak Hebrew.

- **Most people** in the Middle East are Muslims, but Lebanon has many Christians and Israel is mostly Jewish.

- **Many of the Arab** countries of the Middle East – except Israel – are dominated by Islamic traditions.

▲ *Many people in the Middle East wear traditional Arab head coverings.*

- **Islamic countries** of the Middle East are often ruled by kings and emirs, sultans and sheikhs who have absolute power. Yemen is a socialist republic; Turkey and Israel are republics. Iraq is a republic but it is ruled by President Saddam Hussein with absolute power.

> **···FASCINATING FACT···**
> Agriculture was developed in the Middle East around 10,000 years ago.

▲ *A Bedouin wedding party. Although a Saudi husband is considered head of his family, the wife has much authority in running the household.*

- **The Jews of Israel** are locked in a conflict with the Arab people which dates back thousands of years.

- **The people of the United Arab Emirates** (UAE) are among the richest in the world, with a yearly income of almost $20,000 each.

- **The people of Yemen** are among the poorest in the world, with a yearly income of just $270 each.

Afghanistan and neighbours

- **Afghanistan:** Capital: Kabul. Population: 20.5 million. Currency: Afghani. Language: Pashto, Dari.

- **Tajikistan:** Capital: Dushanbe. Population: 5.5 million. Currency: Rouble. Language: Tajik.

- **Kyrgyzstan:** Capital: Bishkek. Population: 4.2 million. Currency: Som. Language: Kyrgyz.

- **Nepal:** Capital: Kathmandu. Population: 21.1 million. Currency: Nepalese rupee. Language: Nepali.

▼ *The Himalays form a barrier that separates northern India from the plateau of Tibet, China.*

- **Tibet:** Capital: Lhasa. Population: 24.1 million. Tibet is not an independent state, but part of China.

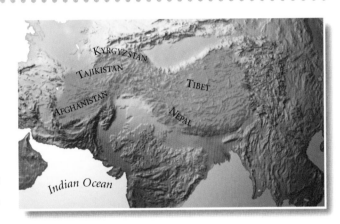

- **These five countries** contain most of the world's highest mountains, including Everest (8846 m) and Kanchenjunga (8598 m) in Nepal and Garmo in Tajikistan (7495 m).

▲ *These five countries are perched on top of the world's highest mountains, the Himalayas.*

- **The brilliant blue** gemstone lapis lazuli has been mined at Sar-e-Sang in Afghanistan for over 6000 years.

- **Kyrgyzstan** has been independent from the USSR since 1991, but many people are Russian or half-Russian. Only a few still live in the traditional kyrgyz tents or 'yurts'.

- **Tajikistan** is still mostly rural, unlike Kyrgyzstan, and farmers in the deep valleys grow cotton and melons.

- **Afghanistan** was wracked by civil war until the fiercely Muslim Taliban came to power in the late 1990s and forced on the people a very harsh regime.

123

Pakistan and Bangladesh

- **Pakistan:** Capital: Islamabad. Population: 144.1 million. Currency: Pakistan rupee. Language: Urdu.

- **Bangladesh:** Capital: Dhaka. Population: 122.7 million. Currency: Taka. Language: Bengali.

- **The Punjab** region is where many Pakistanis live. It gets its name – which means 'five waters' – from five tributaries of the River Indus: the Jhelum, Chenab, Ravi, Sutlej and Beas. These rivers water the Punjab's plains and make it fertile. All the same, large areas of the Punjab are dry and rely on one of the world's biggest irrigation networks.

- **Pakistan's major exports** include textiles, cement and machine tools.

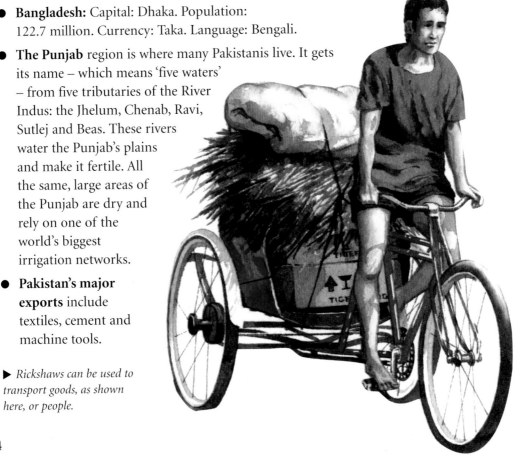

▶ *Rickshaws can be used to transport goods, as shown here, or people.*

- **Buses, lorries and rickshaws** in Pakistan are decorated with colourful patterns, pictures of film stars and religious themes. Many people think that the better the vehicle looks, the more careful the driver will be.

Pakistan

Bangladesh

- **Pakistan's capital** is the brand new city of Islamabad, built in the 1960s, but its biggest city and industrial centre is the port of Karachi.

- **While people in India** are mainly Hindu, in Pakistan and Bangladesh they are mainly Muslim.

- **Jute is a reed** that thrives in Bangladesh's warm, moist climate. It is used for making rope, sacking and carpet backing.

- **Over 70 big jute mills** make jute Bangladesh's most important export.

- **Most of Bangladesh** is low-lying and prone to flooding. Floods have devastated Bangladesh several times in the past 40 years.

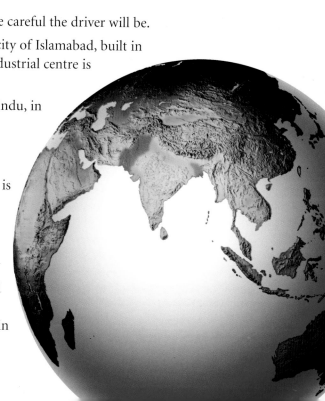

India

- **Capital:** New Delhi. Area: 3,287,263 sq km. Currency: Indian rupee. Languages: Hindi and English.

- **Physical features:** Highest mountain: Kanchenjunga (8598 m). Longest river: Ganges (2510 km).

 ▲ *Hindus consider the Ganges the most sacred river in India. Each year, thousands of pilgrims bathe in the river and take home some of its water.*

126

- **Population:** 1 billion. Population density: 284/sq km. Life expectancy: men 62.3 years; women 62.9 years.

- **Wealth:** GDP: $357.4 billion. GDP per head: $370.

- **Exports:** Gems, jewellery, clothes, cotton, textiles, tea, engineering goods.

- **India has heavy** monsoon rains for six months of the year and dry weather for the rest.

- **India is the world's** largest democracy.

- **Two-thirds** of India's population grow their own food, mainly rice and wheat.

- **India's wheat production** has doubled since the Green Revolution of the 1960s when high-yield hybrids were introduced – but much wheat is sold abroad, pushing prices too high for many poor Indians.

- **India is the world's** tenth biggest industrial nation. Textiles remain important, but there is a growing emphasis on heavy industry, including iron and steel, vehicles, machine tools and pharmaceuticals.

◀ *Hindu women in India traditionally wear beautifully coloured wraps or saris made of fine cloth such as silk.*

Indian food

▲ *Indian food often uses a range of spices in order to create a particular sauce for each dish.*

● **Most Indians** live on very plain diets – based on staples such as rice in the east and south, chapatis (flat wheat bread) in the north and northwest, and bajra (millet bread) in the Maharashtra region.

● **The staple foods** are supplemented by dal (lentil porridge), vegetables and yoghurt.

● **Chillis and other spices** such as coriander, cumin, ginger and turmeric add flavour.

- **Chicken and mutton** are costly and eaten occasionally. Hindus will not eat beef and Muslims will not eat pork.

- **Most Indian meals** are cooked in ghee (liquid butter). Ghee is made by heating butter to boil off water, then allowing it to cool and separate. Ghee is scooped off the top.

- **Although many Indians** have simple diets, India has an ancient and varied tradition of fine cooking.

- **Curries are** dishes made with a sauce including the basic Indian spices – turmeric, cumin, coriander and red pepper. The word curry comes from the Tamil *kari*, or sauce.

▲ *An Indian meal is rarely served on a single plate. Instead, it comes in different dishes, which diners dip into.*

- **The basis of a curry** is a masala, a mix of spices, often blended with water or vinegar to make a paste.

- **Southern Indian** vegetable curries are seasoned with hot blends such as *sambar podi*.

- **Classic northern Indian** Mughal dishes are often lamb, or chicken based, and seasoned with milder garam masala.

129

China

- **Capital:** Beijing. Area: 9,560,900 sq km. Currency: Yuan. Language: Mandarin.

- **Physical features:** Highest mountain: Qomolanjma (Mt Everest, 8848 m). Longest river: Chang (Yangtse) (6300 km).

▲ *China produces about one third of the world's rice.*

- **Population:** 1244.2 million. Population density: 127/sq km. Life expectancy: men 67.9 years; women 72 years.

- **Wealth:** GDP: $902 billion. GDP per head: $860.

- **Exports:** Machinery, clothing, crude oil, tobacco, grains, fish products.

- **China** is the world's third largest country, stretching from the soaring Himalayas in the west to the great plains of the Huang (Yellow) and Chang (Yangtse) rivers in the east where most people live.

- **China** is the most highly populated country in the world. In 1979, it was growing so rapidly the government made it illegal for couples to have more than one child. In the countryside, people disliked the law because extra children were needed to work the fields.

- **70%** of China's people still live and work on the land. But as China opens up to western trade, so industry is growing in cities like Guangzhou (Canton) and more and more country people are going to work there.

> **...FASCINATING FACT...**
> A baby is born in China every two seconds, and someone dies every two and a half.

- **China** became communist in 1949, and the nationalist government fled to the island of Taiwan. China and Taiwan still disagree over who should govern China. Taiwan now has its own thriving economy and makes more computer parts – especially microchips – than any other country in the world.

▶ *With over 1200 million inhabitants, China has more people than any other country. One in five people alive today are Chinese. China is also one of the world's oldest civilizations and Chinese cities date back at least 3500 years. People were farming here long before the pharaohs came to power in Egypt.*

131

Chinese food

- **The staple foods** in China are rice and wheat with corn, millet and sorghum. In the south, the people eat more rice. In the north, they eat more wheat, as bread or noodles.

- **Vegetables** such as cabbage, bean and bamboo shoots are popular. So too is tofu (soya bean curd).

- **Favourite meats** in China are pork and poultry, but the Chinese also eat a lot of eggs, fish and shellfish.

- **A Chinese breakfast** may be rice and vegetables or rice porridge and chicken noodle soup or sweet pastries.

- **A Chinese lunch** may include egg rolls or meat or prawn dumplings called *dim sum*.

▲ *Chinese food has many textures, including slippery mushrooms and crunchy vegetables.*

...**FASCINATING FACT**...
The Chinese were drinking tea at least 4000 years ago.

132

- **A Chinese main meal** may be stir-fried vegetables with bits of meat or seafood in a stock, with rice or noodles.

- **China has** a long tradition of fine cooking, but styles vary. Cantonese cooking in the south has lots of fish, crabs and prawn. Huaiyang has steamed dishes. Szechuan is spicy. Beijing cooking in the north is the most sophisticated, famous for its Peking duck (cripsy roast duck) and Mongolian Hotpot.

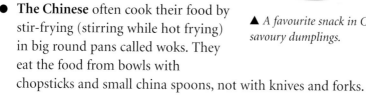

▲ *A favourite snack in China is fried savoury dumplings.*

- **The Chinese** often cook their food by stir-frying (stirring while hot frying) in big round pans called woks. They eat the food from bowls with chopsticks and small china spoons, not with knives and forks.

- **Chinese** drink tea without milk, typically made from jasmine leaves, oolong (green tea) or chrysanthemum.

133

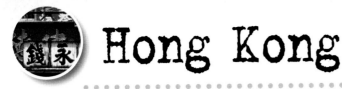

Hong Kong

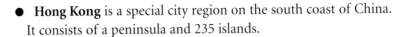

- **Hong Kong** is a special city region on the south coast of China. It consists of a peninsula and 235 islands.

- **Hong Kong** was administered by the British from 1842 until July 1 1997.

- **Over six million** people are crowded into Hong Kong, mostly in the cities of Kowloon and Hong Kong itself.

- **Hong Kong** is one of the world's most bustling, dynamic, overcrowded cities. It makes huge amounts of textiles, clothing and other goods and is also one of the world's major financial and trading centres.

> ... FASCINATING FACT ...
> The proposed Landmark tower in Kowloon could be 574 m tall.

▼ *The Shanghai Bank in Hong Kong. Hong Kong is a centre of international trade and finance.*

▲ *Hong Kong's streets are hectic, with its large population travelling by public transport or cars. Neon-lit advertising signs can be seen everywhere.*

- **All but 2%** of Hong Kong people are Chinese, but many speak English as well as Chinese.

- **Hong Kong** is one of the world's three biggest ports, along with Rotterdam and Singapore.

- **Hong Kong** is the world's biggest container port.

- **Hong Kong's Chep Lap Kok** airport, opened in 1998, is one of the world's most modern airports.

- **The Hong Kong-Shanghai Bank** tower is one of the world's most spectacular modern office blocks.

North and South Korea

- **North Korea:** Capital: Pyongyang. Population: 23 million. Currency: Won. Language: Korean.

- **South Korea:** Capital: Seoul. Population: 45.7 million. Currency: Won. Language: Korean.

North Korea

- **Korea** split into the communist North and capitalist South in 1948.

- **A bitter war** between North and South involving the USA ended with a treaty in 1953.

South Korea

- **North and South Korea** both still have large armies. South Korea's has over half a million soldiers.

- **After the war** money from US banks helped the South become the world's fastest growing economy.

- **Huge factories** run by companies called chaebol churned out everything from computers to Hyundai and Daewoo cars.

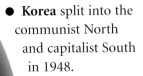

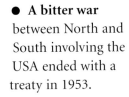

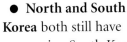

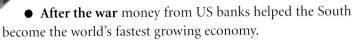

136

- **South Korean shipyards** build one in six of the world's ships. Only Japan builds more.
- **In 1997** North Korea suffered food shortages after two years of floods followed by drought.
- **In 1997-98** the uncovering of massive government dishonesty made many South Korean businesses bankrupt. New President Kim Dae Jung has led a recovery.

▼ *Seoul is one of the world's largest cities with a population of over 12 million. It is the centre of South Korea's cultural, economic and financial activity.*

Japan

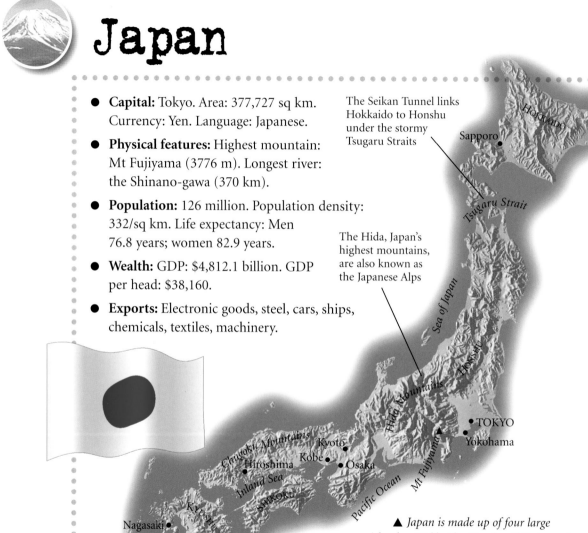

- **Capital:** Tokyo. Area: 377,727 sq km. Currency: Yen. Language: Japanese.

- **Physical features:** Highest mountain: Mt Fujiyama (3776 m). Longest river: the Shinano-gawa (370 km).

- **Population:** 126 million. Population density: 332/sq km. Life expectancy: Men 76.8 years; women 82.9 years.

- **Wealth:** GDP: $4,812.1 billion. GDP per head: $38,160.

- **Exports:** Electronic goods, steel, cars, ships, chemicals, textiles, machinery.

The Seikan Tunnel links Hokkaido to Honshu under the stormy Tsugaru Straits

The Hida, Japan's highest mountains, are also known as the Japanese Alps

HOKKAIDO

Sapporo

Tsugaru Strait

Sea of Japan

Honshu

Hida Mountains

• TOKYO

Yokohama

Chugoku Mountains

Kyoto

Hiroshima • Kobe

• Osaka

Inland Sea

SHIKOKU

Pacific Ocean

Mt Fujiyama

Kyushu

Nagasaki •

▲ Japan is made up of four large islands – Hokkaido, Honshu, Shikoku and Kyushu – and nearly 4000 smaller ones, stretching over almost 2000 km of the western Pacific Ocean. Since the late 20th century, Kyushu, Honshu, Shikoku and other islands are now linked by bridges and tunnels.

● **Japan** is very mountainous, so the big cities where nine out of ten people live are crowded into the coastal plains. 30 million people are crammed into Tokyo and its suburbs alone, making it the biggest urban centre in the world. Tokyo and the nearby cities have tall skyscrapers to make the most of the limited space available – but also with deep foundations, because Japan is prone to earthquakes.

● **Japan** is famous for its electronic goods – including walkmans and games consoles. It also makes huge amounts of steel, half the world's ships and more cars than any other country.

● **All but 15%** of the land is too steep for farming, but millions of little square rice fields are packed onto the coastal plains and on hillside terraces.

● **Most Japanese live** a very modern way of life. But traditions still survive and there are many ancient Buddhist and Shinto shrines.

▲ *The beautiful, snow-capped Mt Fujiyama is the most famous of Japan's 2w000 volcanoes and is sacred to the Shinto religion.*

· · ·**FASCINATING FACT**· · ·
Japan has the world's largest fishing industry with 400,000 vessels catching 12 million tonnes of fish a year.

Tokyo

▲ *Delicate cherry blossom, here seen in Shinjuku Park, Tokyo, traditionally symbolises the great natural beauty of Japan.*

- **Tokyo** is part of the world's largest urban area. With the port of Yokohama and the cities of Chiba and Kawasaki, it makes an urban area that is home to almost 30 million people.

- **Tokyo** is Japan's capital and leading industrial and financial centre.

- **Tokyo's stock exchange** is one of the world's three giants, along with London and New York.

- **Tokyo** was originally called Edo when it first developed as a military centre for the Shoguns. It was named Tokyo in 1868 when it became imperial capital.

- **14,000 people** live in every square kilometre of Tokyo – twice as many as in the same area in New York.

- **Some hotels** in Tokyo have stacks of sleeping cubicles little bigger than a large refrigerator.

▲ *Tokyo is perhaps the busiest, most crowded city in the world.*

- **During rush hours** *osiyas* (pushers) cram people on to commuter trains crowded with ten million travellers a day.

> ...**FASCINATING FACT**...
> Tokyo probably has more neon signs
> than any other city in the world.

- **Traffic police** wear breathing apparatus to cope with traffic fumes.

- **Tokyo mixes** the latest western-style technology and culture with traditional Japanese ways.

Thailand and Burma

- **Thailand:** Capital: Bangkok. Population: 59.7 million. Currency: Baht. Language: Thai.

- **Burma:** Capital: Rangoon. Population: 44.6 million. Currency: Kyat. Language: Burmese.

- **In 1990** the National League for Democracy (NDL) led by Aung San Suu Kyi won free elections in Burma but the army has kept them out of power ever since.

- **Burma's military** leaders call the country Myanmar.

- **Growing opium poppies** to make the painkiller morphine and the drug heroin is one of the few ways the people of north Burma can make money.

- **The world's best rubies** come from Mogok in Burma.

- **Thailand's capital** is called Bangkok by foreigners but its real name has over 17 words beginning 'Krungthep', so many locals call it Krung Thep.

- **Most people in Thailand** and Burma still live in the countryside growing rice to eat.

- **Most people** live on fertile plains and deltas – around the Irrawaddy River in Burma and the Chao Phraya in Thailand.

- **Millions** of tourists come to Thailand each year to visit the country's beaches, and the attractions of the city of Bangkok.

◀ *Many canals thread through Bangkok and provide a way for poor people to bring goods to sell.*

Vietnam and neighbours

- **Vietnam:** Capital: Hanoi. Population: 72.5 million. Currency: New dong. Language: Vietnamese.

- **Laos:** Capital: Vientiane. Population: 4.6 million. Currency: Kip. Language: Lao.

- **Cambodia:** Capital: Phnom Penh. Population: 10 million. Currency: Riel. Language: Khmer.

- **Indonesia:** Capital: Jakarta. Population: 194 million. Currency: Rupiah. Main language: Bahasa Indonesia.

- **Laos, Vietnam and Cambodia** were once French colonies and the end of French rule in the 1950s led to years of suffering and war.

- **Both Laos and Vietnam** are one-party communist states, although their governments are elected by popular vote. In Cambodia, the king was restored to power in 1993.

- **Many people** in Laos and Vietnam are poor and live by growing rice. Laos is the world's poorest country.

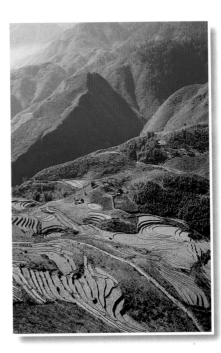

▲ *Cultivated fields near the highest mountain of Vietnam, Sapa.*

144

▲ *Haylong Bay, Vietnam. A beautiful coastline with sandy beaches stretches the length of the eastern side of the country.*

- **In Indonesia,** an elected president has replaced dictator General Suharto but the military still have great power.

- **Spread over 13,677 islands,** Indonesia is one of the world's most densely populated countries. Jakarta is home to seven million, and is heavily industrialized. In the country hillside terraces ensure every inch is used for rice.

- **Indonesian rainforest** is being rapidly destroyed by loggers. In 1997, the country was engulfed by smoke from fires started by loggers.

▲ *Warm and damp, Southeast Asia is a fertile region where Buddhist and Hindu kings once built giant temples in the forests, but many people today are desperately poor.*

145

Malaysia and Singapore

- **Malaysia:** Capital: Kuala Lumpur. Population: 21 million. Currency: Malaysian dollar (ringgit). Language: Bahasa Malaysia.

Malaysia   Singapore

- **Singapore:** Capital: Singapore. Population: 3.4 million. Currency: Singapore dollar. Languages: English, Mandarin, Malay and Tamil.

- **Malaysia** is split into sections: peninsular Malaysia and Sarawak and Sabah on the island of Borneo.

- **In the 1980s** Malaysia was a farming country relying on rubber for exports.

- **Malaysia** is still the world's top rubber producer.

- **Cheap, skilled labour** and oil have turned Malaysia into one of the world's most rapidly developing economies – as the new skyscrapers in Kuala Lumpur show.

▲ *Singapore is one of the busiest and most prosperous cities in Asia. It is home to more than 90% of the country's population.*

146

- **A plan called 2020 Vision** aims to have Malaysia fully developed by the year 2020.

- **Singapore** may be the world's busiest port. Huge ships tie up here every three minutes, day and night.

- **Singapore** is also one of Asia's most successful trading and manufacturing centres.

- **Singapore** has a state-of-the-art transport system, kept immaculately clean by strict laws governing litter.

▼ *Theau Hou Temple, Kuala Lumpar, is one of the largest Chinese temples in Southeast Asia.*

Peoples of southern Asia

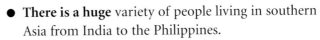

- **There is a huge** variety of people living in southern Asia from India to the Philippines.

  - **India** has hundreds of different ethnic groups speaking 30 languages and 1500 dialects.

  - **Indonesia** also has many different ethnic groups and over 250 different languages.

  - **In Cambodia,** Vietnam, Thailand, Burma and Sri Lanka, people are mostly Buddhists.

  - **In Indonesia,** Malaysia, Pakistan and Bangladesh, people are mostly Muslim.

  - **In India,** 83% of people are Hindus.

  - **The word Hindu** comes from the Indus river where Dravidian people created one of the world's great ancient civilizations 4500 years ago.

  - **By Hindu tradition** people are born into social classes called castes. Members of each caste can only do certain jobs, wear certain clothes and eat certain food.

◀ *Most Vietnamese, like this girl, have broad faces, high cheekbones and straight black hair. However, the population is varied with about 1.25 million Tay, one million Thai, one million Chinese and 900,000 Khmer.*

▶ *At Wat Phra Keo, the Royal Temple in the Grand Palace, Bangkok.*

- **Most Indians** are descended from both the Dravidians and from the Aryans who invaded and pushed the Dravidians into the south about 3500 years ago.

- **The people of East Timor** in Indonesia are mainly Christian. Before they became independent they were under the oppressive rule of the Indonesian military government.

◀ *About 95% of Thai people are Buddhists. This ancient Buddhist temple is in Ayuthaya, about 75 km north of Bangkok.*

149

Pacific food

- **Most places** around the Pacific are near the sea, so fish plays an important part in diets.

- **In Japan** fish is often eaten raw in thin slices called *sashimi*, or cooked with vegetables in batter as a dish called *tempura*, often served with soy sauce.

- **At home** most Japanese eat traditional foods including rice and noodles, as well as fish, tofu and vegetables or eggs.

- **When out,** many Japanese people eat American-style foods from fast food restaurants.

- **The Japanese** eat only half as much rice now as they did in 1960, as younger people prefer bread and doughnuts.

- **Younger Japanese** people have a diet richer in protein and fat than their parents', so grow eight to ten cm taller.

- **Pacific islanders** traditionally ate fish such as bonito and tuna and native plants such as breadfruit, coconuts, sweet potatoes and taro. They made flour from sago palm pith.

- **Many islanders** now eat nothing but canned Western food and suffer malnutrition.

◄ *Lightly grilled or barbecued giant prawns and other seafood play a major role in Pacific food.*

- **Philippino** food is a mix of Chinese, Malay, American and Spanish. Adobo is chicken and pork in soy sauce.

- **Some Australians** now often eat 'fusion' food which blends Asian with European cooking styles.

▼ *A woman prepares breadfruit ready for eating in Kiribati, North Tarawa.*

151

North Africa

- **Morocco:** Capital: Rabat. Population: 26.9 million. Currency: Dirham. Language: Arabic.

- **Algeria:** Capital: Algiers. Population: 29.4 million. Currency: Algerian dinar. Language: Arabic.

- **Tunisia:** Capital: Tunis. Population: 9.2 million. Currency: Tunisian dinar. Language: Arabic.

- **Libya:** Capital: Tripoli. Population: 5.2 million. Currency: Libyan dinar. Language: Arabic.

- **Much of** the world's phosphate supply comes from Morocco and Tunisia.

- **Algeria, Libya and Tunisia** all have large reserves of oil and gas.

- **People in Morocco,** Tunisia and Algeria eat a lot of couscous. Couscous is made from wheat which is pounded into hard grains of semolina, then steamed until soft. The couscous is then served with stewed lamb or vegetables.

◀ *This colosseum is a legacy of Roman rule over Tunisia. The Romans held power here from 146 BC until AD 439 when the Vandals invaded.*

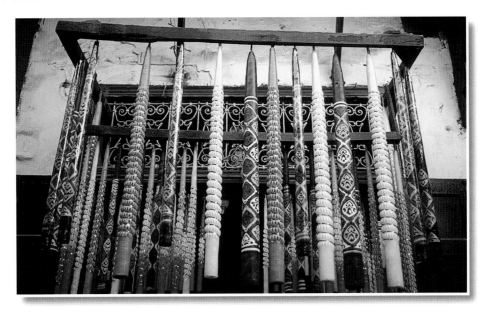

▲ *Wonderfully ornate goods, such as these candles, can be found in the Moroccan cities of Fez and Marrakesh.*

- **The Moroccan** custom is to eat using the left hand rather than with knives and forks.

- **The historic cities** of Fez and Marrakesh in Morocco are famous for their colourful souks or markets, where thousands of tourists each year come to haggle over beautiful hand-woven carpets, leather goods and jewellery.

. . . **FASCINATING FACT** . . .
Libya is building the 600 km Great Manmade River, the world's longest water pipe, to supply towns in the desert.

153

Egypt and neighbours

- **Egypt:** Capital: Cairo. Population: 64.7 million. Currency: Egyptian pound. Language: Arabic.

- **Ethiopia:** Capital: Addis Ababa. Population: 58.2 million. Currency: Ethiopian birr. Language: Amharic.

- **Sudan:** Capital: Khartoum. Population: 27.7 million. Currency: Sudanese dinar. Language: Arabic.

- **Egypt relies** heavily on tourists visiting its ancient sites, such as the 4700 year-old Great Pyramid of Cheops at Giza.

◀ *The Sultan Hassan mosque, Cairo, dates from the mid-1300s and is an outstanding example of Muslim architecture.*

154

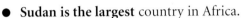

- **99% of Egyptians** live by the River Nile which provides water for farming, industry and drinking. The world's largest reservoir, Lake Nasser, was created when the Nile was dammed by the Aswan High Dam.

- **Cairo** has a population of ten million and is growing so rapidly there are major housing and traffic problems.

- **Lots of cotton** is grown in Egypt and the Sudan.

- **Sudan is the largest** country in Africa.

- **In the 1980s and 1990s** the people of Ethiopia, Sudan and Somalia suffered dreadful famine. Many people here are still very poor and without enough to eat.

- **Grasslands south of the Sahara** are dotted with acacia thorn trees which ooze a liquid called gum arabic when their bark is cut. This was used

▼ *The pyramids, great tombs for the dead, were built on the edge of the desert near the river Nile.*

West Africa

▲ *Ivory Coast alone grows a third of the world's cocoa beans. Here beans are drying in the sun.*

- **West African countries** are: Mauritania, Mali, Burkina Faso, Senegal, Gambia, Guinea Bissau, Liberia, Guinea, Ivory Coast, Ghana, Sierra Leone, Togo, Benin and São Tomé and Prîncipe. All have populations under ten million except for Ghana, Ivory Coast and Mali.

- **Ghana:** Capital: Accra. Population: 18.7 million. Currency: Cedi. Language: English.

- **Ivory Coast:** Capital: Yamoussoukro. Population: 13.6 million. Currency: CFA franc. Language: French.

Ghana

Ivory Coast

Mali

- **Mali:** Capital: Bamako. Population: 10.4 million. Currency: CFA franc. Language: French.

- **West Africa** grows over half the world's cocoa beans.

- **Yams** are a vital part of the diet of people in West Africa.

- **West Africa** is rich in gold and diamonds, which once sustained the ancient civilization of Mali and its famous capital of Timbuktu.

- **Ghana and Guinea** are rich in bauxite (aluminium ore).

- **Ghana** was called Gold Coast by Europeans because of the gold offered by the Ashanti peoples there.

- **Ghana** is still poor, but under President Rawlings, many of its young people are the best educated in Africa.

▲ *Yams are a staple food and are often eaten at breakfast, dinner and tea.*

Nigeria and neighbours

▲ *The baobab is an African tree that grows in the savannas. Its massive trunk can store water, and it produces large, edible, pulpy fruit.*

- **Nigeria:** Capital: Abuja. Population: 103.9 million. Currency: Naira. Language: English.

- **Niger:** Capital: Niamey. Population: 9.8 million. Currency: CFA franc. Language: French.

158

- **Chad:** Capital: N'Djamena. Population: 7.1 million. Currency: CFA franc. Languages: Arabic and French.

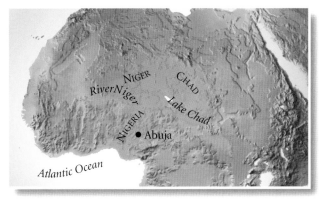

- **Most people** in the north of Nigeria, and in Niger and Chad, live by growing food for themselves.

- **The amount of rainfall** increases dramatically from north to south, and the vegetation changes from desert to dry grassland to rainforest in marked bands.

▲ *The position of Nigeria, Niger and Chad on the southern fringes of the Sahara desert makes them prone to drought as climate change and overgrazing push the desert further south.*

- **In the dry north** people grow mainly millet; in the moist south, they grow rice and roots such as cassava and yam, which they eat boiled with goat, chicken and fish.

- **Oil makes up 98%** of Nigeria's exports.

- **The money from oil** has made Nigeria among the most heavily urbanized and populous countries in Africa, especially around its main city Lagos.

- **Nigeria** is home to over 250 different peoples.

- **Nigeria** became a democracy again in 1998 after years of bitter civil war and military dictatorship, but tensions remain.

Central Africa

- **Equatorial Guinea:** Capital: Malabo. Population: 400,000. Currency: CFA Franc. Language: Spanish.

- **Gabon:** Capital: Libreville. Population: 1.1 million. Currency: CFA franc. Language: French.

- **Congo (Brazzaville):** Capital: Brazzaville. Population: 2.6 million. Currency: CFA franc. Language: French.

- **Cameroon:** Capital: Yaoundé. Population: 12.8 million. Currency: CFA Franc. Language: French and English.

- **Central African Republic (CAR):** Capital: Bangui. Population: 3.4 million. Currency: CFA Franc. Language: French.

- **French and English** are official languages, but most people speak their own African language.

- **Most Gabonese** are farmers, but Gabon is rich in iron and manganese and famous for its ebony and mahogany wood.

- **75% of people** in Cameroon are farmers, growing crops such as cassava, corn, millet, yams and sweet potatoes. Most of Cameroon's roads are dust roads.

▲ Cameroon, Gabon, CAR, Congo and Equatorial Guinea lie near the Equator, and are often thickly wooded with rainforest.

- **Congo (Brazzaville)** is so called to distinguish it from neighbouring Congo (Kinshasa). It is the one of the world's poorest countries. It is thickly forested and many people travel by dugout canoes. Many raise bananas or grow crops to feed themselves.

- **The CAR and Equatorial Guinea** are perhaps the least developed countries in Africa.

▼ *As Cameroon has shortages of teachers many children do not attend school. Only about 40% of 15 year-olds or above can read or write.*

Congo (Kinshasa)

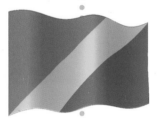

- **Capital:** Kinshasa. Area: 2,344,880 sq km. Currency: New zaire. Language: French.

  - **Physical features:** Highest mountain: Margherita Peak (5109 m). Longest river: Congo (4667 km).

  - **Population:** 48 million. Population density: 20/sq km. Life expectancy: men 52 years; women 56 years.

- **Wealth:** GDP: $5.2 billion. GDP per head: $108.

- **Exports:** Copper, cobalt, diamonds, coffee, petroleum.

▲ *Industrial diamonds are mined in Congo.*

◀ *Coffee is an important 'cash crop': it is grown to be sold abroad rather than to feed Congo's own population.*

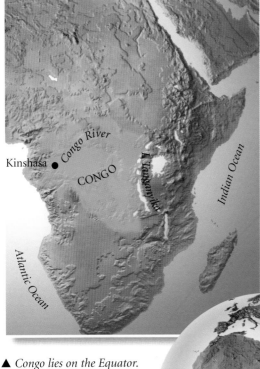

▲ *Congo lies on the Equator. Over a third of it is thick equatorial rainforest.*

● **Congo** is called Congo (Kinshasa) or Democratic Republic of Congo to distinguish it from a neighbouring country also called Congo, Congo (Brazzaville).

● **From 1885 to 1971** Congo was a Belgian colony known as the Belgian Congo. From 1971 to 1997 it was called Zaire.

● **Congo** is one of the world's leading copper producers. There is a vast copper mine in Shaba (once called Katanga) in the southeast.

● **Congo is** the world's leading industrial diamonds producer.

● **The Congo River** is the world's eighth longest river, and carries more water than any river but the Amazon.

163

Kenya

- **Capital:** Nairobi. Area: 582,646 sq km. Currency: Kenyan shilling. Languages: Swahili and English.

- **Physical features:** Highest mountain: Mt Kenya (5199 m). Longest river: Tana (800 km).

- **Population:** 33.8 million. Population density: 50/sq km. Life expectancy: men 51.1 years; women 53 years.

- **Wealth:** GDP: $9.7 billion. GDP per head: $340.

- **Exports:** Tea, coffee, fruit, flowers, vegetables, petroleum products.

- **Remains of early human ancestors** found by Lake Turkana show people have lived in Kenya for millions of years.

▲ *The Masai people of Kenya are just one of about 50 ethnic groups in Kenya. Their brightly coloured neck bands and jewellery are usually saved for special ceremonies.*

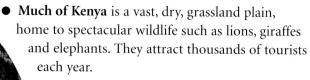

● **Much of Kenya** is a vast, dry, grassland plain, home to spectacular wildlife such as lions, giraffes and elephants. They attract thousands of tourists each year.

  ● **Most Kenyans** live on small farm settlements, raising crops and livestock for themselves, but there are big cash crop plantations for tea, coffee, vegetables and flowers.

  ● **Many Kenyans** are moving to the big cities: Nairobi and Mombasa.

  ● **Kenya's population** is growing rapidly – by 3% a year.

▼ *Nairobi possesses an important snake park where creatures such as this East African bush snake can be found.*

East Africa

- **Tanzania:** Capital: Dodoma. Population: 28.8 million. Currency: Shilling. Languages: English and Swahili.

- **Rwanda:** Capital: Kigali. Population: 7.7 million. Currency: Franc. Languages: French and Kinyarwanda.

- **Burundi:** Capital: Bujumbura. Population: six million. Currency: Franc. Languages: French and Kurundi.

- **Uganda:** Capital: Kampala. Population: 20.6 million. Currency: Shilling. Language: English and Swahili.

- **Malawi:** Capital: Lilongwe. Population: 11.1 million. Currency: Kwacha. Languages: Chichewa and English.

- **A fifth of Malawi** is taken up by Lake Nyasa, one of the world's largest, deepest lakes and home to the usipa, a sardine-like fish that in dried form provides the people of Malawi with their main protein.

◀ *Tanzania is famous for safaris in the Serengeti park where lions, elephants, giraffes and many other animals are seen.*

▲ *The grasses of the savannas provide food for grazing animals such as giraffes. Gazelles, zebras and many birds and insects also live here.*

- **The countries** of East Africa are the least urbanized in the world, with nine out of ten people living in the countryside.

- **In 1994** Rwanda and Burundi were ravaged by the worst genocide in African history as tribal war flared between the Tutsi and Hutu peoples.

- **Lake Victoria** on the Tanzania and Uganda border covers 69,484 sq km, one of the world's largest lakes.

- **One of Tanzania's** main crops is sisal, a kind of palm. Sisal leaves are crushed to extract fibre to make rope.

Southern Africa

◄ *Houses near Lobit: about three-quarters of Angolans live in rural areas.*

- **Mozambique:** Capital: Maputo. Population: 18.4 million. Currency: Metical. Language: Portuguese.

- **Angola:** Capital: Luanda. Population: 11.7 million. Currency: Kwanza. Language: Portuguese.

- **Zambia:** Capital: Lusaka. Pop: 8.6 million. Currency: Kwacha. Language: English.

- **Population:** Namibia: 1.6 million. Botswana: 1.5 million. Swaziland: 966,000.

- **Large areas** of southern African countries are too dry to farm intensively. Most people grow crops such as maize or raise cattle to feed themselves.

- **In Mozambique** plantations grow crops such as tea and coffee for export, but most people who work on them are poor.

- **In 2000** much of Mozambique was devastated by huge floods from the Zambezi and Limpopo Rivers.

- **Zambia is the** world's fourth largest copper producer and relies on copper for 85% of its export earnings.

- **Namibia is one of the** world's largest lead producers.

- **Namibia has the** world's biggest uranium mine and an estimated three billion carats of diamond deposits.

▼ *The Namib desert lies along southern Africa's west coast. It has the highest sand dunes in the world – some are more than 400 m tall.*

Zimbabwe

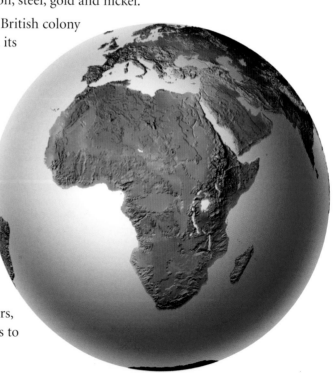

- **Capital:** Harare. Area: 390,759 sq km. Currency: Zimbabwe dollar. Language: English.

- **Physical features:** Highest mountain: Mt Inyangani (2595 m). Longest river: Zambezi (2700 km).

- **Population:** 11.3 million. Population density: 28/sq km. Life expectancy: men 43.6 years; women 44.7 years.

- **Wealth:** GDP: $8.2 billion. GDP per head: $720.

- **Exports:** Cigarettes, cotton, steel, gold and nickel.

- **Zimbabwe** was once the British colony of Rhodesia but declared its independence in 1980.

- **The name Zimbabwe** came from the huge ancient stone palace of Great Zimbabwe (which means 'house of the chief').

- **Zimbabwe** is a fertile farming country, growing lots of tobacco, cotton and other crops. Much of the land still remains in the hands of white farmers, but the government plans to change this situation.

▶ *Victoria Falls on the Zambezi is one of the world's biggest waterfalls. Its roar can be heard 40 km away.*

● **Zimbabwe** is the most industrial African nation after South Africa, making steel, cement, cars, machines, textiles and much more. The industrial centre is Bulawayo.

● **98% of Zimbabweans** are black. The Shona people are the biggest group, then come the Ndebele (or Matabele). The Shona speak a language called Chishona, the Ndebele speak Sindebele.

171

South Africa

- **Capital:** Pretoria. Area: 1,225,815 sq km. Currency: Rand. Languages: nine African languages including Zulu, plus English and Afrikaans.

- **Physical features:** Highest mountain: Champagne Castle (3375 m). Longest river: the Orange (2173 km).

- **Population:** 38.8 million. Population density: 31/sq km. Life expectancy: men 51.5 years; women 58.1 years.

- **Wealth:** GDP: $130.2 billion. GDP per head: $3210.

- **Exports:** Gold, diamonds, metals, metal products, machinery, citrus fruit, wine.

- **Until 1991** people of different races in South Africa were separated by law. This was called apartheid.

- **Apartheid** meant many black people were forced to live in specially built townships such as Soweto. Townships are far from cities and workplaces, so workers must commute for hours each day on crowded buses.

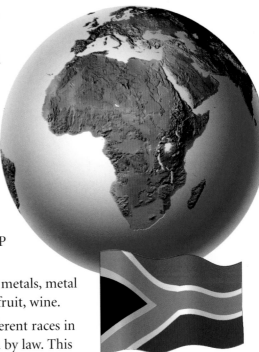

◀ *Nelson Mandela was the hero of the struggle against apartheid in South Africa. In 1994 he became the country's first president elected by all the people.*

...FASCINATING FACT...
In the 1900s, almost half the world's
gold came from South Africa.

▲ *Johannesburg is the largest city in
South Africa with a population of
about four million.*

- **South Africa** has three capital cities. The administration is in Pretoria, the courts are in Bloemfontein and parliament is in Cape Town.

- **South Africa** produces more diamonds than all of the rest of the world put together.

173

Peoples of Africa

- **Africa has been** inhabited longer than any other continent. The earliest human fossils were found here.

- **In the north** in countries such as Algeria, Morocco and Egypt, people are mainly Arabic.

- **The Berber people** were the first people to live in northwest

▲ *These Gambians are celebrating with drumming and dancing. There are five main ethnic groups in Gambia: the Mandingo, Fula, Wolof, Serahuli and Jola.*

Africa, with a culture dating back to at least 2400 BC. Their culture survives in remote villages in the Atlas mountains of Algeria and Morocco.

- **Tuaregs** are camel-herding nomads who live in the Sahara desert, but much of their traditional grazing land has been taken over by permanent farms.

- **South of the Sahara** most people are black Africans.

- **There are more than 800** ethnic groups of black Africans.

- **Over 1300** different languages are spoken in Africa, more than any other continent.

▼ *The Tuareg are the largest group of nomads living in the Sahara. More than 300,000 live here, mainly in Algeria, Mali and Niger.*

- **Most people** in southern Africa speak English or one of 100 Bantu languages such as Zulu or Swahili.

- **Many people** in rural southern Africa live in round houses.

- **Africa was ruled** by the Europeans as colonies. By the early 20th century the country was divided into nations. Many small groups became dominated by tribes and cultures perhaps hostile to their own.

Australia

- **Capital:** Canberra. Area: 7,682,300 sq km. Currency: Australian dollar. Language: English.

- **Physical features:** Highest mountain: Mt Kosciusko (2228 m). Longest river: the Darling (2739 km).

- **Population:** 18.3 million. Population density: 2/sq km. Life expectancy: men 75.5 years; women 81.1 years.

- Wealth: GDP: $394 billion. GDP per head: $20,650.

▲ *New South Wales rears almost one-third of Australia's sheep.*

- **Exports:** Ores and minerals, coal, oil, machinery, gold, diamonds, meat, wool, cereals.

- **Australia** is the only country that is also a continent.

- **Most of Australia** is so dry only 2% is good for growing crops, although the country sells a lot of wheat. But huge areas are used for rearing cattle and sheep, many raised on vast farms called 'stations'. Australia is also famous for its wines.

- **Australia has huge amounts** of iron, aluminium, zinc, gold and silver. The Mount Goldsworthy mine in Western Australia alone is thought to have 15 billion tonnes of iron ore. Broken Hill in New South Wales is the world's largest silver mine.

- **Australia's mild climate** encourages outdoor activities such as surfing. Thousands head for Bondi Beach near Sydney on Christmas Day for a party or to surf. Australia is also the world's top cricketing nation.

► *Australia is the world's smallest continent but sixth biggest country. Much of it is dry and thinly populated. Most people live in the southeast or along the coast.*

Darwin
Arnhem Land
Gulf of Carpentaria
Kimberley Plateau
Great Barrier Reef
Great Sandy Desert
QUEENSLAND
Great Artesian Basin
Alice Springs
Lake Eyre
Brisbane
WESTERN AUSTRALIA
Flinders Ranges
Perth
Great Australian Bight
CANBERRA
Sydney
Adelaide
Mt Kosciusko ▲
Melbourne
Bass Strait
The railtrack across Nullabor Plain is the world's longest straight track
TASMANIA
Hobart
The Great Dividing Range divides the moist coastal plain from the dry outback

...FASCINATING FACT...
Australia's 140 million sheep produce more than a third of the world's wool.

177

Australian landmarks

▲ *Uluru is sacred to the Aboriginals. On its surface and in its caves are paintings made long ago by Aboriginal artists.*

- **Australia's most famous landmark** is Uluru or Ayers Rock, the biggest monolith (single block of stone) in the world, 348 m high and 9 km around.

- **Uluru** is the tip of a huge bed of coarse sand laid down in an inland sea some 600 million years ago.

- **Lake Eyre** is Australia's lowest point, 15 m below sea level. It is also Australia's biggest lake by far, but it is normally dry and fills only once every 50 years or so.

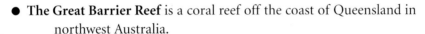

- **Nullarbor plain** is a vast, dry plain in southern Australia. Its name comes from the Latin *nulla arbor* ('no tree').

- **Shark Bay** is famous for its sharks and dolphins.

- **Shark Bay** is also famous for its stromatolites, the world's oldest fossils, dating back 3.5 billion years. These are pizza-like mats made by colonies of blue-green algae.

- **The Darling River** is Australia's longest river (2739 km long), but it only flows in summer.

- **The Great Barrier Reef** is a coral reef off the coast of Queensland in northwest Australia.

    - **The Great Barrier Reef** is the world's biggest coral reef, over 2000 km long.

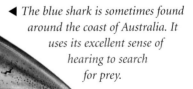

◀ *The blue shark is sometimes found around the coast of Australia. It uses its excellent sense of hearing to search for prey.*

....FASCINATING FACT...
The Great Barrier Reef is the world's largest structure made by living things.

Peoples of Australia

- **The Aborigines** make up 1.5 % of Australia's population today, but they were the first inhabitants.

- **The word aborigine** comes from the Latin *ab origine*, which means 'from the start'.

- **Aborigine cave paintings** and tools have been found in Australia dating back to at least 45,000 years ago.

- **Aborigines** prefer to be called Kooris.

- **British people** began to settle in Australia about 200 years ago. They now form the majority of the population, along with other white Europeans.

- **Many of the earliest** settlers in Australia were convicts, transported from Britain for minor crimes.

▶ *The Kooris or Aborigines of Australia spread right across the Pacific many thousands of years ago and were probably the first inhabitants of America as well.*

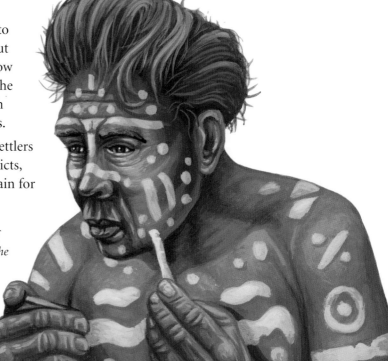

- **Many Australians** have ancestral roots in the British Isles.

- **The British settlers** drove the Aborigines from their land and 60% now live in cities.

- **After hard campaigning** some Aboriginal sacred sites are being returned to them, with their original names. Ayers Rock is now known as Uluru. A famous trial in 1992 returned to Aborigine Eddy Mabo land on Murray Island first occupied by his ancestors before the Europeans arrived.

- **Many recent immigrants** to Australia are from Southeast Asia and Greece.

▼ *Sydney is Australia's biggest and oldest city. Most inhabitants have British ancestry, but other Europeans are settling there, as well as Asians. Several thousand Aborigines live there too.*

New Zealand

- **Capital:** Wellington. Area: 270,534 sq km. Currency: NZ dollar. Language: English.

- **Physical features:** Highest mountain: Mt Cook (3764 m). Longest river: Waikato (425 km).

- **Population:** 3.8 million. Population density: 14/sq km. Life expectancy: men 74.1 years; women 79.7 years.

- **Wealth:** GDP: $59.5 billion. GDP per head: $15,830.

- **Exports:** Meat, milk, butter, cheese, wool, fish, fruit.

- **New Zealand** was one of the last places to be inhabited by humans and remains a clean, beautiful land, with rolling farmland, thick forests and towering mountains.

- **New Zealand** is mainly a farming country, with over 50% of the land devoted to crops and pasture for sheep and cattle. 75% of New Zealand's exports are farm produce.

- **Fast-flowing** rivers provide 75% of New Zealand's power through hydroelectric plants. Geothermal energy from hot springs provides some of the rest. Nuclear power is banned.

▲ *New Zealand is a place of unspoilt natural beauty and much of the countryside is protected by national parks.*

● **The first** inhabitants of New Zealand were the Maoris, who came about AD800 and now form 13% of the population. The remaining 87% are mostly descended from British settlers who came in the 19th and 20th centuries.

The Pacific Islands

▲ *Like many Pacific islands, Fiji seems like a paradise.*

- **Scattered** around the Pacific are countless islands – maybe 20,000 or 30,000. Some are little more than rocks; some are thousands of square kilometres.

- **The Pacific Islands** altogether are sometimes known as Oceania, but they are in three main groups: Melanesia, Micronesia and Polynesia.

- **Melanesia** includes New Guinea, the Solomons, New Caledonia, Vanuatu and Fiji.

- **Melanesia** means 'black islands' and gets its name from the dark skin of many of the islanders here.

- **Micronesia** is 2000 islands to the north of Melanesia, including Guam and the Marshall Islands.

- **Micronesia** means 'tiny islands'.

- **Polynesia** is a vast group of islands 8000 km across. It includes Tahiti and Easter Island.

- **Polynesia** means 'many islands'.

- **Most of the islands** in the Pacific are either extinct volcanoes, or coral islands built around a volcanic peak. Atolls are coral rings left as the volcano sinks.

- **Most Pacific islanders** still live in small farming or fishing villages as they have for thousands of years, but western influences are changing the island way of life rapidly.

▶ *There are more than 500 of these enormous stone carvings of human heads on Easter Island. Some are up to 21 m high.*

185

Antartica

- **Antarctica** is the fifth largest continent, larger than Europe and Australia, but 98% of it is under ice.

- The **Antarctic population** is made up mostly of scientists, pilots and other specialists there to do research in the unique polar environment.

- **About 3000 people** live in Antarctica in the summer, but less than 500 stay all through the bitter winter.

- **The biggest community** in Antarctica is McMurdo which is home to 2000 people in summer and has cafés, a cinema, a church and a nuclear power station.

- **People and supplies** reach McMurdo either on ice-breaker ships that smash through the sea ice, or by air.

- **McMurdo settlement** was built around the hut the British polar explorer Captain Scott put up on his 1902 expedition to the South Pole.

- **The Amundsen–Scott** base is located directly underneath the South Pole.

186

- **Antarctica** has a few valuable mineral resources including copper and chrome ores.

- **There is coal** beneath the Transarctic Mountains, and oil under the Ross Sea.

- **Under the Antarctic Treaty** of 1961, 12 countries agreed a ban on mining to keep the Antarctic unspoiled. They allow only scientific research.

◀ *Emperor penguins are among the few large creatures that can survive the bitter Antarctic winter. They breed on the ice cap itself.*

187

Population

- **The world's population** climbed above 6 billion in 1999.

- **Over a quarter** of a million babies are born every day around the world.

- **World population** is growing at a rate of about 1.6% per year.

- **At the current rate** world population will hit 10 billion by 2020.

- **Between 1950** and 1990, the world's population doubled from about 2.5 billion to 5 billion, adding 2.5 billion people in 40 years.

▲ *China will continue to control the growth of its population in the 21st century. Its goal is to keep the number below 1.4 billion until 2010.*

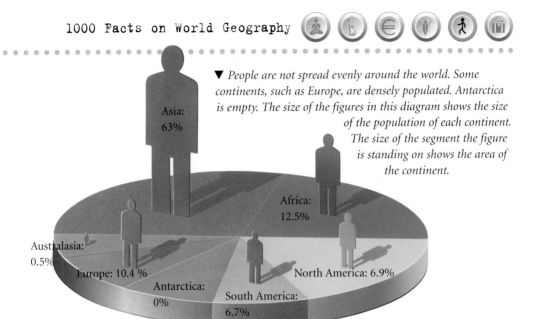

▼ *People are not spread evenly around the world. Some continents, such as Europe, are densely populated. Antarctica is empty. The size of the figures in this diagram shows the size of the population of each continent. The size of the segment the figure is standing on shows the area of the continent.*

Asia: 63%

Africa: 12.5%

Australasia: 0.5%

Europe: 10.4 %

Antarctica: 0%

South America: 6.7%

North America: 6.9%

- **The 1990s** added a billion people. The next decade will add 1.5 billion. This adds 2.5 billion in 20 years.

- **Asia has** about 60% of the world's population. China alone has 1.3 billion people and India has 1 billion.

- **The number of babies** born to each woman varies from 1.15 in Spain to 7.6 in Yemen.

- **Latvia** has 100 women to every 85.3 men; Qatar has 197.8 men every 100 women.

- **In the developed world** people are living longer. In Japan people expect to live 80 years on average. In Sierra Leone, people only live 37.2 years.

189

Rich and poor

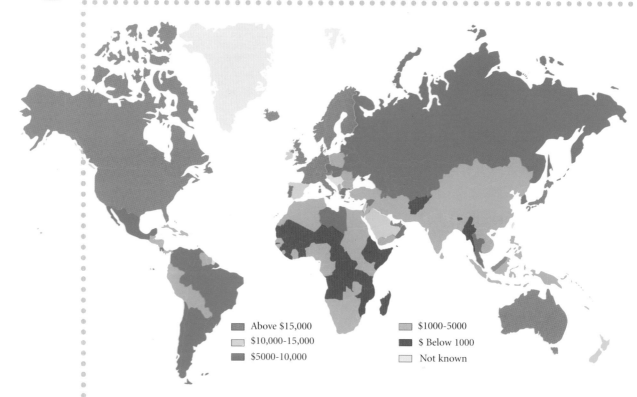

Above $15,000
$10,000-15,000
$5000-10,000
$1000-5000
$ Below 1000
Not known

▲ *One of the clearest ways of seeing the huge gap in wealth between countries is by looking at the gross domestic product (GDP) per head. This is what a person would get if the country's entire income was split up equally among everyone. This map shows the GDP per head for all the world's countries.*

● **The world's richest country** is the USA, with a GDP of $7783 billion. But people in Switzerland have an even higher GDP per head – $43,060.

- **The world's poorest country** by GDP per head is Burma (Myanmar). Each person has, on average, $100, but many people are even poorer.

- **The world's richest countries** with less than a quarter of the world's population take three-quarters of its wealth.

- **Most of the world's rich countries** are in the Northern Hemisphere. Most poor countries are in the South. So people talk of the North-South divide.

- **One billion people** around the world live in 'absolute poverty'. This means they have no real homes. In cities, they sleep rough or live in shacks. They rarely have enough to eat or drink.

- **In the 1970s** richer countries encouraged poorer countries such as Mexico and Brazil to borrow money to build new dams and industrial works.

- **By 1999** poor countries were paying $50 billion more in debt interest than rich countries were donating in aid.

- **Famine** has become a common problem in the poorer parts of the world. One reason is that so much farmland is used for growing crops for export – raising the cost of food, and restricting the land available for growing food for local people.

- **250,000** children die a week from a poor diet. 250,000 die a month from diarrhoea, because of a lack of clean water.

> **. . . FASCINATING FACT . . .**
> About half a billion people are starving
> or don't get enough to eat.

Industry

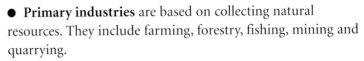

- **Primary industries** are based on collecting natural resources. They include farming, forestry, fishing, mining and quarrying.

- **Things made** by primary industries are called primary products or raw materials.

- **Primary industries** dominate the economies of poorer countries. Copper is 85% of Zambia's exports.

- **Primary products** are much less important in developed countries. Primary products earn just 2% of Japan's GDP.

- **Secondary industry** is taking raw materials and turning them into products. This is called manufacturing and processing.

- **Tertiary industries** are the service industries that provide a service, such as banking or tourism, not a product.

◀ *Banking is one of the most important service industries. The biggest and most powerful banks are worth billions of pounds.*

▲ *The coal-fired Fiddlers Ferry Power Station, Cheshire, UK, can produce enough electricity to meet the peak needs of about two million people.*

- **Tertiary industry** has grown enormously in the most developed countries, while manufacturing has shrunk.

- **'Postindustrialization'** means developing service industries in place of factories.

- **Tertiary industries** include internet businesses.

...**FASCINATING FACT**...
More than 70% of the UK's income now comes from tertiary industry.

World Trade

- **International trade** is the buying and selling of goods and services between different countries.

- **International trade** has increased so much people talk of the 'globalization' of the world economy. This means that goods are sold around the world.

- **The balance of world trade** is tipped in favour of the world's richest countries and companies.

- **Just 200 huge multinational** companies control much of world trade.

- **Just five countries** – the USA, Germany, Japan, France and the UK – control almost half world trade.

- **The 23 richest countries** control 74% of world trade.

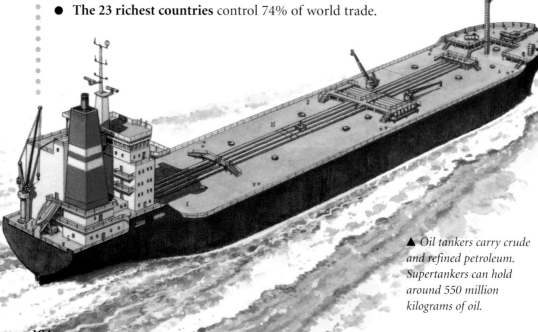

▲ *Oil tankers carry crude and refined petroleum. Supertankers can hold around 550 million kilograms of oil.*

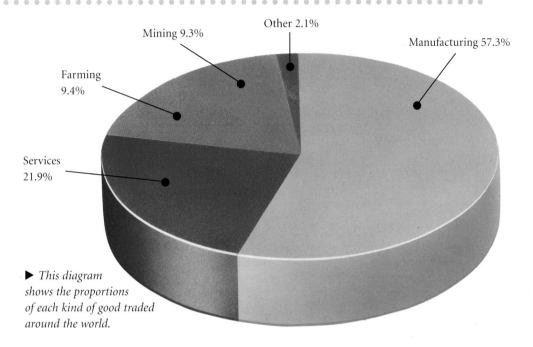

Other 2.1%

Mining 9.3%

Manufacturing 57.3%

Farming 9.4%

Services 21.9%

▶ *This diagram shows the proportions of each kind of good traded around the world.*

- **The 40 poorest countries** control just 5% of world trade.

- **Some countries** rely mainly on just one export. 98% of Nigeria's export earnings come from oil; 80% of Ghana's come from cocoa.

- **Some countries** want 'free trade' – that is, no restrictions on trade; other less powerful nations want tariffs (taxes on foreign goods) and quotas (agreed quantities) to protect their home industries.

- **The World Trade Organization** was founded on January 1, 1995 to police world trade, and to push for free trade.

International organizations

- **International organizations** are of three main types: those set up by governments, such as the UN; multinationals; and human rights and welfare organizations such as the Red Cross and Amnesty International.

- **The United Nations** or UN was formed after World War II to maintain world peace and security. It now has over 160 member nations.

- **UN headquarters** are in New York City. The name was coined by US President Roosevelt in 1941.

- **All UN members** meet in the General Assembly. It has five permanent members (Russia, USA, China, France and UK) and ten chosen every two years.

- **The UN** has agencies responsible for certain areas such as children (UNICEF), food and farming (FAO), health (WHO), science (UNESCO) and nuclear energy (IAEA).

- **Multinationals** or TNCs (transnational corporations) are huge companies that work in many countries.

- **TNCs** such as Coca-Cola and Kodak are well known; others such as cigarette-makers Philip Morris are less known.

- **Some TNCs** take in more money than most countries. Just 500 TNCs control 70% of all the world's trade.

▲ *The Red Cross flag was a tribute to Switzerland, home of the organization's founder.*

▲ *The Red Cross was set up by Swiss Jean Dunant in the 19th century after he witnessed the bloody slaughter at the battle of Solferino in Italy. It now plays a vital role in helping suffering people everywhere.*

- **90% of world grain** is handled by six big US TNCs. Cargill and Continental alone control half the world's grain.

- **Amnesty International** was founded in 1961 to campaign for those imprisoned for religious and political beliefs.

197

Political systems

- **Democracies** are countries with governments elected every few years by popular vote.

- **Most democracies** have a constitution, a written set of laws saying how a government must be run.

- **Democracies** such as France are republics. This means the head of state is an elected president. In some republics such as the USA, the president is in charge; in others, the president is a figurehead and the country is run by a chancellor or prime minister.

- **Monarchies** are countries which still have a monarch – a king or queen – like Britain. But their power is usually limited and the country is run by an elected government.

- **In autocracies** a single person or small group of people hold all the power, as in China and North Korea.

- **Most governments** are split into the legislature who make or amend laws, the executive who put them into effect and the judiciary who see they are applied fairly.

◀ *Elizabeth II became queen of Britain in 1952 at the age of 25. Prince Charles is the next in line.*

▶ *Bill Clinton was President of the USA from 1992–2000.*

- **Most countries** are capitalist, which means most things – capital – are owned by individuals or small groups.

- **A few countries** such as Cuba are communist, which means everything is owned by the community, or rather the state.

- **Socialists** believe the government should ensure everyone has equal rights, a fair share of money, and good health, education and housing.

- **Fascists** believe in rigid discipline and that they and their country are superior to others, like Hitler's Germany in the 1930s. There is no openly fascist country at present.

▶ *Leader of the Labour Party, Tony Blair was elected Britain's Prime Minister in 1997.*

World Religions

▲ *Praying to Kaaba, the most sacred shrine of Islam.*

● **Christianity** is the world's largest religion, with 1.5 billion followers. Christians believe in a saviour, Jesus Christ, who lived in Israel 2000 years ago. Christ, they believe, was the Son of God. When crucified (nailed to a wooden cross), he rose from the dead to join God in heaven.

● **Islam** is the world's second largest religion with 1.3 billion believers. It was founded in Arabia in the 7th century by Mohammed, who Muslims believe was the last, greatest prophet sent by *Allah* (Arabic for God). The word *Islam* means 'submission' and Muslims believe they must obey God totally and live by the holy book The Koran.

● **Hinduism** is 4000 years old. Hindus worship many gods, but all believe in *dharma*, the right way to live. Hindus believe we have past lives. By following *dharma*, we may reach the state of *Moksha* and never be re-born again.

● **Christianity** is split into three branches: Catholics whose leader is the Pope in Rome; Protestants; and the Eastern Orthodox church. Islam is split into Sunnis and Shi'ites. Shi'ites are the majority in Iraq and Iran.

● **Buddhism** is the religion of 300 million Asians. It is based on the teachings of Prince Siddhartha Gautama, who lived in India from 563 to 483 BC.

● **Judaism** is the religion of Jews. They were the first to believe in a single god, who they called *Yahweh*, over 4000 years ago. There are over 11 million Jews living outside Israel and 3.5 million living in Israel.

> ....**FASCINATING FACT**....
> The Hindu holy text, the Mahabharata, is the longest poem ever written, with around 200,000 verses.

▶ *Each major religion except for Christianity is concentrated in one part of the world. Islam, for instance, is practised mainly in western Asia, the Middle East and North Africa. Hinduism is the major religion in India. Buddhism is practised widely in Southeast Asia, especially China, Tibet, Thailand and Cambodia. Christianity is the exception. Most Christians live in Europe, Australia and the Americas, but the religion was spread around the world by European colonists and missionaries.*

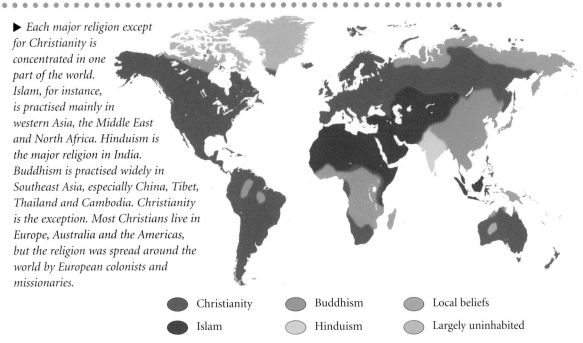

● Christianity   ● Buddhism   ● Local beliefs
● Islam   ● Hinduism   ● Largely uninhabited

- **Most of the world's** major religions except for Hinduism are monotheistic – that is, they believe in just one God.

- **Three million Muslims** visit their holy city of Mecca in Saudi Arabia every year on pilgrimage.

- **Jains of India** will not take any form of life. They eat neither meat nor fish, nor, usually, eggs. Jain priests often sweep paths in front of them as they go to avoid stepping on insects.

201

Health and education

- **Progress** in medical science, better diet and improved hygiene have made the world a healthier place for many.

- **How long** people are likely to live is called life expectancy. In 1950, the world average was just 40 years. Now it is over 63 years.

- **Life expectancy** is usually high in richer countries. The Japanese live, on average, for 80 years; the Swiss live for 78 years.

- **Life expectancy** is much lower in poor countries. People in Sierra Leone live just 37.2 years; people in Malawi live 39.3 years.

- **Vaccination programmes** have reduced the effects of some major diseases. The terrible disease smallpox was thought to be wiped out in 1977.

- **Some diseases** are on the increase in poorer parts of the world. AIDS (Acquired Immune Deficiency Syndrome) is now killing huge numbers of Africans.

- **In some parts** of the world, disease, lack of food and water, and poor healthcare mean that one child in every four dies before reaching the age of five in poor countries such as Afghanistan and Sierra Leone.

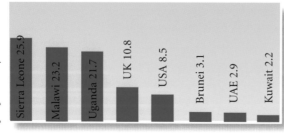

◀ *Death rates per thousand people vary from over 20 in many African countries to under three in many Arab countries of the Gulf.*

- **In the USA and Europe** less than one child in a hundred dies before the age of five.

- **In wealthier** countries such as the USA and Japan, there is on average one doctor for every 400 people.

- **In most poor African** countries, there is just one doctor for every 50,000 people.

▶ *The first vaccination ever was given in 1796 by Edward Jenner. He used cowpox matter to vaccinate against smallpox.*

Energy

- **Humans** now use well over 100 times as much energy as they did 200 years ago.

- **Europe, North America and Japan** use 70% of the world's energy with just a quarter of the people.

- **Fossil fuels** are coal, oil and natural gas – fuels made from organic remains buried and fossilized over millions of years. Fossil fuels provide 90% of the world's energy.

- **Fossil fuel** pollutes the atmosphere as it burns, causing health problems, acid rain and also global warming.

Food for living

Industry | Home | Transport

◀▼ Each person in developed countries uses ten times as much energy as each person in less developed countries.

Energy use in developed countries | Energy use in less developed countries

- **Fossil fuel** is non-renewable. This means it can't be used again once burned. At today's rates, the world's coal and oil will be burned in 60 years and its natural gas in 220 years.

- **Renewable energy** such as running water, waves, wind and sunlight will not run out. Nuclear energy is non-renewable, but uses far less fuel than fossil fuel.

- **Alternative energy** is energy from sources other than fossil fuels and nuclear power. It should be renewable and clean.

- **Major alternative energy** sources are waves, geothermal, tides, wind and hydro-electric power.

- **The Sun** provides the Earth with a vast amount of energy. At the moment only a tiny fraction of this is used.

> ...**FASCINATING FACT**...
> The average American uses 340 times as much energy as the average Ethiopian.

Oil is our most important energy source, providing almost 40% of the world's energy. The biggest reserves are around the Caspian Sea and the Middle East.

Coal still provides almost 30% of the world's energy needs. Two-thirds of the world's reserves are in China, Russia and the USA. India and Australia are major producers too.

Wood and dried animal dung – called biomass – provide the main fuel for half the world's population. In some poorer countries, it provides 90% of all fuel.

Natural gas provides over 20% of world energy needs, and the proportion is rising. The biggest reserves are in Russia, the USA and Canada.

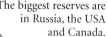

Hydrolectric power (HEP) uses fast-flowing rivers or water flowing through a dam to generate electricity. HEP supplies 7% of world energy needs.

Nuclear power now provides about 5% of the world's energy needs. The major producers are France, the USA and Russia.

Geothermal power uses heat from deep inside the Earth – either to heat water or make steam to generate electricity. Experts think geothermal use will go up.

Windpower, wavepower and solar energy produce barely 5% of the world's energy needs. The proportion is going up, but only very, very slowly.

▲ *The pie diagram in the centre shows how much of the world's energy is provided by different sources. The top layer shows proportions ten years ago. The bottom layer shows proportions now. See how biomass energy use has risen.*

Agriculture

- **Only 11%** of the Earth's ice-free land surface is suitable for growing crops – that is, about 13 billion hectares. The rest is either too wet or dry or cold, or has soil that is too shallow or poor in nutrients.

- **A much higher** proportion of Europe has fertile soil (36%) than any other continent. About 31% is cultivated.

- **In North America** 22% of the land is fertile but only 13% is cultivated, partly because much fertile land is lost under concrete. Surprisingly, 16% of Africa is potentially fertile, yet only 6% is cultivated.

- **Southern Asia** is so crowded that even though less than 20% of the land is fertile, over 24% is cultivated.

- **Dairy farms** produce milk, butter and cheese from cows in green pastures in fairly moist parts of the world.

- **Mixed farming** involves both crops and livestock as in the USA's Corn Belt, where farmers grow corn to feed pigs and cattle.

▲ *In places farming is now a highly mechanized industry, but in SE Asia many farmers work the land as they have for thousands of years.*

- **Mediterranean farming** takes place in areas with mild, moist winters and warm, dry summers – such as California, Australia and the Mediterranean. Winter crops include wheat and barley. Summer crops include citrus fruits and olives.

- **Shifting cultivation** involves growing crops such as corn, rice, manioc, yams and millet in one place for a short while, then moving on before the soil loses goodness.

- **Shifting cultivation** is practised in the forests of Latin America, in Africa and in Southeast Asia.

▶ Most of the world's food is grown in the Northern Hemisphere or Asia. Asia is the main grower of wheat, rice, sweet potatoes, sorghum and all pulses such as beans. In fact, 90% of all rice and sweet potatoes are grown in Asia. Half the world's corn is grown in North America. 40% of potatoes are grown in Europe.

Millet
Oats
Barley
Potato
Rice

Maize
Casava
Wheat
Sweet Potato
Soya Bean

. . . FASCINATING FACT . . .
There are now over twice as many farm animals in the world as humans – over 14 billion.

Index

Index

Index

Index

Index

Index

Index

Index

Acknowledgements

The publishers would like to thank the following artists
who have contributed to this book:

Nicholas Forder, Mike Foster, Terry Gabbey, Jeremy Gower, Rob Jakeway,
John James, Kevisn Madison, Terry Riley, Martin Sanders, Mike Saunders,
Rob Sheffield, Mike White, John Woodcock

The publisher would like to thank the following sources for the use
of their photographs:

CORBIS: Page 12 Catherine Karnow; Page 51 Jeffrey L. Rotman;
Page 80; Adrian Arbib; Page 120 Hanan Isachar; Page 156 Eye Ubiquitous

All other pictures from the Miles Kelly Archives